PRAISE FOR *THE ORGANICALLY CLEAN HOME*

"I have been a fan of using 'green' cleaners for quite some time now, but I have found that they are typically either extremely expensive to purchase or extremely time-consuming to make. Being a busy mom to three boys, it is always my goal to find ways to simplify as many areas of our lives as possible. The recipes in this book allow me to do just that with my cleaning routine and desire to remain organic. I feel at ease knowing exactly what is going into my cleaners, and that many of the recipes can be made with just a few simple ingredients. The best part is that this book not only contains family-friendly solutions for our everyday tasks, but also solutions for those 'surprise' cleaning sessions as well!"

—Jennifer Jones, IHeart Organizing (*http://iheartorganizing.blogspot.com*)

"Clean Mama brings a breath of fresh air to cleaning, literally. Packed full of nontoxic recipes, tips, and checklists, this book is sure to become a well-loved reference manual in any home."

—Toni Hammersley, A Bowl Full of Lemons (*www.abowlfulloflemons.net*)

"*The Organically Clean Home* is a wonderful resource for anyone struggling to find a manageable home-cleaning routine. I found the cleaning schedules and printables to be very well done and particularly useful. Also, the bounty of all-natural cleaning recipes here is truly remarkable! As a mom with three young children running around, I love that I now have a nontoxic way to clean virtually everything in my home—no more worrying about what my little ones are ingesting as I'm scrambling to clean up after them. I'd highly recommend this book to parents and nonparents alike."

—Stephanie Morgan, Modern Parents, Messy Kids (*www.modernparentsmessykids.com*)

PRAISE FOR *THE ORGANICALLY CLEAN HOME*

"If you want to start using safe, homemade cleaning products, *The Organically Clean Home* is a must-have resource. Becky will teach you how to make every cleaning product needed to clean your home from top to bottom, plus implement a routine that will *keep* your home clean too!"

—Christine Satterfield, i Dream of Clean (*www.idreamofclean.net*)

"*The Organically Clean Home* is a very thorough book that teaches you why it's important to clean organically, and gives you tons of recipes to get you started. It made me take a second look at what I use to clean my home and opened my eyes to a whole new world of homemade organic cleaning products!"

—Anna Moseley, Ask Anna (*www.askannamoseley.com*)

The Organically
CLEAN HOME

The Organically
CLEAN HOME

150 Everyday Organic Cleaning Products You Can
Make Yourself—The Natural, Chemical-Free Way

Becky Rapinchuk, *www.cleanmama.net*

Aadamsmedia
Avon, Massachusetts

Published by
Adams Media, a division of F+W Media, Inc.
57 Littlefield Street, Avon, MA 02322. U.S.A.
www.adamsmedia.com

ISBN 10: 1-4405-7251-8
ISBN 13: 978-1-4405-7251-7
eISBN 10: 1-4405-7252-6
eISBN 13: 978-1-4405-7252-4

Printed in the United States of America.

10 9 8 7 6 5 4 3

Library of Congress Cataloging-in-Publication Data

Rapinchuk, Becky.
  The organically clean home / Becky Rapinchuk, www.cleanmama.net.
    pages cm
  Includes bibliographical references and index.
  ISBN-13: 978-1-4405-7251-7 (pb : alk. paper)
  ISBN-10: 1-4405-7251-8 (pb : alk. paper)
  ISBN-13: 978-1-4405-7252-4 (ebook)
  ISBN-10: 1-4405-7252-6 (ebook)
1. House cleaning–Environmental aspects. 2. Cleaning compounds–Environmental aspects. 3. Natural
products. 4. Formulas, recipes, etc. I. Title.
  TX324.R37 2014
  648'.5–dc23
                              2013045804

Many of the designations used by manufacturers and sellers to distinguish their product are claimed as
trademarks. Where those designations appear in this book and F+W Media, Inc. was aware of a trademark
claim, the designations have been printed with initial capital letters.

Cover design by Sylvia McArdle.
Cover image © Adams Media.
Interior icons © iStockphoto.com/dutchicon/TheresaTibbetts.

Readers are urged to take all appropriate precautions before undertaking any how-to task. Always read
and follow instructions and safety warnings for all tools and materials, and call in a professional if the task
stretches your abilities too far. Although every effort has been made to provide the best possible information
in this book, neither the publisher nor the author is responsible for accidents, injuries, or damage incurred as
a result of tasks undertaken by readers. This book is not a substitute for professional services.

This book is available at quantity discounts for bulk purchases.
For information, please call 1-800-289-0963.

ACKNOWLEDGMENTS

A big thank you to my family and friends for your love, support, and prayers—I love you all! Thank you to my wonderful husband, George, and my three babies for putting up with the craziness that comes with writing a book in the midst of real life. This book exists because of God who really truly makes ALL things good in His time.

CONTENTS

CHAPTER 4

RECIPES FOR BATHROOMS 83

CHAPTER 5

RECIPES FOR LAUNDRY 107

CHAPTER 6

RECIPES FOR BEDROOMS AND LIVING SPACES . . 127

CHAPTER 7

RECIPES FOR FLOORS 151

INTRODUCTION

Looking for cheaper and much safer alternatives to the store-bought cleaning products you have under your sink? Look no further! In this book, you'll find 150 recipes for practically *any* cleaning dilemma, from natural disinfection to safe and effective stain removal. With just a few simple (and pronounceable) ingredients, you will be a cleaning scientist on your way to an organically clean home.

Why should you clean organically? You'll be able to clean your entire home, inside and out, with homemade products that are safe to use while your kids and pets are in the same room, and are inexpensive to boot! You'll learn how to make everyday products like an all-purpose cleaner and laundry detergent, but you'll also learn the best and safest way to clean things you don't clean every day, like your carpet and your garage floor. Even better, you can scent your products to your liking with a variety of all-natural essential oils.

Think that natural cleaners won't do as good a job as the commercial versions? Wrong! You'll be pleasantly surprised at how effective natural cleaners are. Homemade cleaners are also easily customizable—I'll show you how to adjust formulas to create the perfect cleaning products for your home and cleaning preferences. Every home is different, but this guide gives a variety of solutions for a variety of conditions, so you're sure to find something that works for your home. Now there's no need to stash and store dozens of bottles of different cleaning products "just in case"—you have the ultimate guide to making any product yourself when you need it!

Are you ready to start making your own cleaning products? Grab this book, gather a few of the recommended all-natural ingredients and cleaning tools, and get started. You won't believe how simple it is to formulate your own cleaning products . . . and better yet, you won't believe the amazing results. As a matter of fact, you might even start looking forward to cleaning your house!

CHAPTER 1

ORGANIC CLEANING
101

It doesn't matter if you're attempting to clean out an entire room or a single drawer, you need time and a plan. Yet for most people, finding the time and an effective cleaning strategy is difficult. Throw in the toxins from store-bought cleaning products, and the whole situation is downright scary. To avoid feeling overwhelmed, check out the cleaning strategies in this chapter. You'll find easy-to-implement routines, timesaving ideas, and basic information on natural cleaners. Instead of being a tedious chore, housecleaning will be a breeze!

CAUTION: These recipes and formulations are organic in nature and nontoxic, but as with any cleaner in your home, keep them out of reach of children and pets. As long as around 1 percent of the cleaner is made up of essential oils (as is true for the recipes in this book), it is generally considered safe for pets, but check with your veterinarian first if you're concerned. Please use care in mixing and follow the intended uses and directions.

Why Use Organic Cleaning Products?

There are many great reasons to switch to organic or natural cleaning products. Maybe you want to . . .

- Keep toxins out of your home. (Most homemade products are toxin-free!) According to the Centers for Disease Control and Prevention, accidental household poisonings affect more than 300 children in the United States every day. If you keep the medicine cabinet locked and use cleaning products that are safe, you're reducing your risk of an accident.
- Save some money. (You certainly will!)
- Cut down on what you're sending to the landfill. (You can cut back dramatically on plastics by simply using reusable spray bottles and cleaning containers.)
- Use natural products because someone in your home has asthma or allergies. (Organic cleaners are much better to use around those with sensitivities.) Interestingly enough, the stuff that you clean with can actually make you sick, essentially negating the benefits of cleaning itself. According to the Environmental Working Group (*www.ewg.org*), conventional cleaning products and artificial fragrances can trigger asthma, can include low levels of 1,4-dioxane (a carcinogen), and can even include low levels of formaldehyde (another carcinogen) without disclosure. These ingredients can also lead to birth defects in pregnant women using the cleaners. Although many people don't have any reactions to the toxins, why take a chance?

No matter why you've decided to use organic cleaning products, you can rest assured that you are cleaning with the safest products and getting the best results at the same time.

THE SAFETY FACTOR

Perhaps the most common reason people choose organic cleaners is that they're safer to have around the house than the store-bought versions. Sadly, safe cleaning products are *not* the norm. You'd think that cleaning products would have to be safe to be sold for home use, but that isn't the always the case. I experienced this firsthand when my oldest child was a toddler and grabbed a "safe" cleaning product (sold to be used on highchairs and baby products) and sprayed it in her face and consequently her mouth. I grabbed the bottle from her hands and washed her off. After a quick glance of the bottle, I realized that a call to poison control was necessary. This incident ended safely with her drinking a cup or two of milk and taking a long bath, but my journey to finding safe cleaning products was just beginning.

Take a look at your cleaning product labels and read the warnings and lists of ingredients. You might see warnings like "hazardous to humans and animals" and "causes substantial but temporary eye injury," and unpronounceable ingredients like "*ethanolamine*" or "*hexoxyethanol.*" Even the ingredient "fragrance" is a concern because it can cause skin irritation, and can trigger asthma and allergies. Scary stuff, right?

CHECK PRODUCT RATINGS

A fantastic resource for determining the safety of products in your home is Environmental Working Group, online at *www.ewg.org*. They rate the safety of just about every over-the-counter brand and product. You'll see that with the exception of borax, most ingredients in this book are an A on an A to F scale. I love a clean house, and I hold high standards for products that I create and endorse. It has to be safe and it has to work. This might seem like an easy accomplishment, but it's not.

Commercial cleaners are composed primarily of water, chemicals, and fragrance. Some of these chemicals can aggravate allergies and skin sensitivities as well as pose poisoning risks to children and pets that may get their hands and paws on them when you aren't looking. Besides the obvious poison risks, breathing in the fumes of some cleaners can also be a health risk. For example, some cleaners say to use a mask or to ventilate a room while using, but most users probably don't follow that safety rule. Even if you do, is that really a product you want to be using in your home?

As someone who is nervous about germs and getting sick (and then having a whole house of sick family members!), I understand the appeal of store-bought products that say they kill 99.9 percent of all bacteria. Killing germs is actually difficult to do, but in a normal household, making sure the surfaces are wiped down daily does get rid of the majority of germs and bacteria. If you want to kill them altogether, there are natural ways to do that with 99.9 percent accuracy, too—you'll find a variety of disinfecting recipes in this book. When I realized that keeping counters clean and wiped down regularly will accomplish the same goal, I began making my own safe and natural cleaning products.

THE COST-SAVINGS FACTOR

If making your own cleaning products isn't appealing enough for safety reasons, you'll actually be able to save money, too! Did you know you can make a bottle of all-purpose cleaner for pennies and you can make a batch of powdered laundry detergent for less than $5? A 16-ounce bottle of homemade granite cleaner costs less than 25 cents, whereas a 16-ounce bottle of granite cleaner at the store is at least $5. That 68-load box of detergent you just heaved into your trunk and paid over $15 for? You can make it for under $5. Actually, with my recipe you'll get a few more loads out of it so it'll be an even better savings. If you purchase your ingredients in larger quantities, you'll be making just about every cleaning product from this book to clean your entire home for mere pennies per use!

The Benefits of a Cleaning Routine

Even with organic cleaners, fitting cleaning into a busy schedule isn't easy. Maybe that's because most of us would rather be doing *anything* besides cleaning. Cleaning is what you put off and get to when you can or when you have absolutely nothing else to do. But it doesn't have to be that way. Finding time each day to squeeze a little cleaning into your schedule is difficult, but for most of us, the benefits far outweigh the alternative—spending an entire day or more cleaning.

The first step to embracing a cleaning routine is to understand what a "clean house" really is. *Spotless* isn't the goal, but *clean* is. People you love live in your home and you want them to fully enjoy life in that place. Clean bathrooms rank pretty high on my priority list, but toys strewn from one end of the living room to the next shows that kids are enjoying themselves. Again: Clean is the goal, not spotless.

It doesn't matter if you are out of the house for 50 hours a week, or home all day, you can accomplish a successful cleaning routine that works for you and your schedule. The important thing is to start somewhere. If you think you're too busy to start a cleaning routine, I'd argue that you're too busy *not* to start a cleaning routine. You probably spend more time complaining about cleaning or dealing with ongoing messes than you would actually cleaning!

I like to keep a few rules in mind as I think about my cleaning routine. If these exact rules don't work for you, they can easily be tweaked for any family.

1. Be realistic. I keep my expectations realistic, and doing this is what has allowed me to maintain the simple routine for years. Big resolutions and changes are rarely kept because they are difficult to sustain over a period of time. Instead, create small and attainable cleaning goals.

2. Put your family first. My family comes before cleaning. If I haven't gotten around to cleaning the bathrooms and the kids want me to go play outside, I don't clean the bathrooms then. The bathrooms will be there tomorrow, but playing outside with the kids won't always be there.

3. Set a short time limit. My goal is to spend 15 to 20 minutes a day cleaning. You might choose to spend 10 minutes a day. Whatever it is, limit yourself and work quickly to accomplish your goal and move on. You might find that you have 5 minutes in the morning before you leave for work to do a little cleaning. Tidy your kitchen and make your bed and head out the door. You'll appreciate the 5 minutes you spent

that morning when you return home at night to a clean kitchen.

4. Remember, perfection is not the goal—comfort, ease, and a fresh, clean home is. Taking time to clean and keep things tidied up will help you enjoy your home without the distraction of a pile of magazines or dirty clothes in the way.

My goal for you is simply to help you start somewhere. Don't get discouraged if you can't complete everything every day—that's what tomorrow is for. And don't waste time and energy trying to invent "the perfect plan."

A Cleaning Routine That Works!

My cleaning philosophy is simple: Every day, I do the same four basic tasks. Then I rotate through other tasks on a daily, weekly, monthly, or seasonal basis.

EVERY DAY

Again, these are not big jobs that take a ton of time. But doing the following four tasks will make your home run more smoothly and will make bigger cleaning jobs easier, because you are keeping up with daily maintenance.

1. Sweep floors. Do a quick sweep of any floors that need it—most likely, the kitchen or mudroom. I have a little mini dustpan and broom hanging in the pantry at kid level so my kids can take care of their crumbs around and under the table. Keep an eye out for pet hair, if that's a problem in your house.

2. Declutter. Perform a *quick* declutter of mail, school papers, toys, clothes, and other odds and ends. This is not the time to clean out a file cabinet; it's for recycling the day's junk mail and putting away Legos. Making a quick pickup part of your daily routine is essential to keeping your wits about you. Make sure other family members are involved as well. Try setting a timer for young children before bed and give them 5 minutes to see how many toys they can put away. Many kids will embrace cleaning when it's a "game" and there's a timer involved.

3. Do a load of laundry. I complete at least one load of laundry every day. That means taking that one load through the *complete* cycle of wash, dry, fold, and put away. (This approach gets rid of laundry baskets at various states of completeness scattered throughout the home.) Doing a load a day might sound overwhelming at first, but it will evolve into a habit, which will in turn free your time and energy for other things. Imagine it: You'll eliminate the piles and piles of laundry that build up when you do it infrequently.

4. Wipe counters. I wash out the kitchen sink every evening with a dishwasher-safe brush and dish soap, then quickly wipe down the kitchen counters. Yes, the kitchen counters may need to be wiped down more than once a day, but putting it on a checklist ensures that it will be done at least once. "Wipe counters" also includes doing a quick check/wipe of bathroom counters. A quick swipe around the bathroom counters can be done in a minute or two and it definitely keeps the weekly bathroom cleaning a little more manageable.

If you are just starting with a cleaning routine, simplify the daily list by doing only a load of laundry and the daily decluttering. Clutter and laundry pile up so quickly, it's important to stay on top of those so you don't get the feeling that you'll never get caught up. Then after a week, add the counters to the mix and get used to that. Once you feel like you have the clutter, laundry, and counters under control, add the final daily task of sweeping the floors.

ONCE A WEEK

Then, every day of the week gets an additional task:

1. MONDAY—Clean Bathrooms: All the bathrooms get cleaned, minus the floors. This includes washing counters, scrubbing showers and/or tubs, and cleaning mirrors and toilets.

2. TUESDAY—Dust: A quick weekly dusting is a 15 to 20 minute task that even little kids can get involved in. I like to use a dusting mitt and a long-handled dusting wand to get all the high corners and spaces. Keeping up with dusting every week is so much easier than dealing with dust buildup so bad that the kids start writing "dust me" on the furniture.

3. WEDNESDAY—Vacuum: Thoroughly vacuum all floors (carpet and hard surfaces). Yes, I sweep daily and spot vacuum as needed throughout the week, but Wednesday is the day that I really concentrate on giving the whole house a good vacuuming. I start with the crevice attachment on the vacuum cleaner to vacuum the edges of the room first. Once this is completed, I move on to vacuum the middle. Vacuum horizontally in each room and then vacuum vertically in each room. Yes, you are going over the carpet twice, but this technique ensures that the carpet is lifted and the dirt that may be embedded is removed. This is especially helpful to remove pet hair and dander. Another good idea is to vacuum from the farthest corner away from the door and vacuum your way out of the room. This will give you those beloved vacuum lines that say, "I just vacuumed."

TAKE VACUUMING UP A NOTCH

Use the carpet neutralizer recipe if your carpet needs a little freshening, or add a cotton ball with a drop or two of your favorite essential oil to the bag or canister to add a little aromatherapy to your vacuuming.

4. THURSDAY—Wash Floors: All hard surface floors get washed— I like to use a steam mop on my vinyl and tile floors. I use vinegar and warm water with a couple of drops of lemon and clove essential oils on my hardwood floors.

5. FRIDAY—Catchall Day: This is a day to focus on what didn't get done earlier in the week. I love having a day of grace built into my schedule. Some Fridays, I complete a monthly or seasonal cleaning task; other Fridays I complete a different home task or do grocery shopping. I just choose the most pressing task or two and tackle them.

6. SATURDAY—Wash Sheets and Towels: Instead of doing "regular" laundry, I concentrate on washing all the towels and sheets on Saturdays. You'll love the powdered laundry detergent recipe for your sheets and towels—it makes them so fresh and soft!

7. SUNDAY—Just the Basics: Sunday is a family day and a day of rest and relaxation for us. I just do the four daily tasks (sweep floors, declutter, do a load of laundry, wipe counters).

This routine helps me stay on top of cleaning without letting it take over my life. I've been doing it so long that it's just part of my life and doesn't feel as daunting as it may in the beginning phase of implementation. My goal is that this guide gets you to the same place: comfortable doing simple, manageable tasks that give you a sense of accomplishment and help your life run more smoothly.

Other Cleaning Tips

Following are some other little things that can make your approach to cleaning simpler and more effective:

Don't go to bed without a clean kitchen. For me, this means cleaning off the counters and kitchen table, hand washing anything that needs it, and having started the dishes in the dishwasher, if it's full. This might sound extreme, but try it. It's great to get up in the morning, make your way into the dark kitchen, and not see a mess ahead of you.

Pick up the family room before bed. Pillows and blankets back on the couch, toys and books put back in their baskets, etc. The kitchen and family rooms are connected in our home, so waking up to two clutter-free rooms gives me the freedom to take my morning a little slower without the added stress of feeling overwhelmed before the day has even begun. The family room is likely a much-used spot in your house, too.

Unload the dishwasher right away in the morning. Instead of watching your coffee brew, unload the dishwasher. Rinse breakfast dishes and put them in the dishwasher right away, instead of stacking them up.

Get other family members involved. Even little ones can be expected to pick up what they've been using or playing with. You'll find this to be helpful in the efficiency of a household and controlling the clutter. Take into consideration your own child's ability level and age, but here are some ideas: help make their beds, put away dirty clothes, pick up toys, feed pets, set the table. My little ones like to use a small dusting wand to help dust low areas; they use baby wipes to wipe the baseboards if I'm cleaning them too, and they use a mini dust pan to sweep up their own mealtime crumbs. Encouraging these small tasks early on will help your children get into the habit of cleaning up after themselves and cleaning up a little bit every day.

Follow the "Touch It Once" rule. Try to put things away without dealing with the same thing more than once. As you bring in your mail, look through it, recycle or shred what can be disposed of, and file the bills in their proper home right away. Try to eliminate putting things somewhere temporarily. Instead, bring them to their proper spot the first time. This is such a simple concept but it can be difficult to implement. Persevere in getting your family on the bandwagon. You will find that it'll make your daily life so much easier.

Now that you have a clear vision as to what the method entails, all you have to do is start somewhere. Every day is a new day—what you didn't complete the day before can be tabled or you can try to accomplish it the next day with the next day's task. Don't forget that Friday is a Catchall Day, intended as a day to catch up on unfinished or uncompleted tasks.

Charting Your Progress

My cleaning routines will stick, I promise. The key is to start. Don't worry about it not working or when you'll get it done, just start. The appendix of this book provides some of my cleaning routines in handy chart form to help you get and stay motivated and organized. Use the WEEKLY CLEANING CHECKLIST to keep yourself on task and on track. Sometimes adding a little check mark to the box when you have completed a task can be all the encouragement you need to feel like you are accomplishing something.

After you've been working with the weekly cleaning routine and checklist and you feel like you are ready to add another layer, take a look at the MONTHLY (ROTATING) CLEANING CHECKLIST. These are tasks that are completed monthly, bimonthly, and quarterly. Decide when these tasks can be incorporated into the rest of your life and routine. I usually incorporate them as I am able to on Fridays. I have also included a blank MONTHLY (ROTATING) CLEANING CHECKLIST in case you'd like to formulate your own.

CHAPTER 2

BUILD YOUR CLEANING KIT

Before you start mixing recipes, it's a good idea to collect some basic equipment and ingredients you'll use frequently. You're likely to own most of these items already—you might even find you have much more than you need. When you simplify your cleaning routine and use organic cleaners, you might find that you can discard some of the "cleaning clutter" you've amassed over the years.

Tools

You probably own a variety of cleaning tools that you use in various parts of your house. Here's a list of standard items you'll want to have on hand to complete any part of your new cleaning routine. Try building small caddies of tools that you can leave in the appropriate room—for example, put a bathroom cleaning caddy filled with the appropriate tools and cleaners under the bathroom sink (equipped with a lock to keep kids and pets away!). That way, your tools are right where you need them.

MICROFIBER CLOTHS

Microfiber cleaning cloths are a polyester and nylon blend of cloth that can be found in a variety of textures and weaves to clean different surfaces. I use microfiber cleaning cloths for cleaning just about every surface in my home. They are my favorite cleaning tool because they don't leave lint or streaks on surfaces, and they can be washed at least 300 times, making them extremely economical. You can also buy microfiber cloths that are specially designed for cleaning windows, stainless steel, and mirrors.

An insider tip: Most of my microfiber cloths are from the automotive section of my favorite big-box store. These are a little larger in size and they are less expensive in this section than the cleaning section!

SCRUB BRUSHES

Designate separate scrub brushes for specific jobs to avoid cross-contamination. For example, use a grout brush for the bathroom and a scrub brush for the kitchen sink. You can even use a toothbrush to scrub small spaces—just make sure you *only* use it for cleaning, of course.

SPRAY BOTTLES

Sixteen-ounce spray bottles will work great for most of the recipes in this book. Buy bottles that you like the look of—they don't have to be boring clear plastic models! If you like your equipment, you'll be more likely to use it. Amazon.com has a great selection of spray bottles, and I frequent the cleaning supply aisle at the local supermarkets and grab cool spray bottles when I see them.

CONTAINERS WITH LIDS

Canning jars or cleaned and reused jelly and sauce jars make attractive storage containers—simply add a cute label and you won't miss your flashy packaging from the store. Keep a little stash of different-size containers on hand for storing your cleaning concoctions.

ICE CUBE TRAYS

Ice cube trays make great forms for cleaning and freshening tablets. Instead of measuring out scoops of dishwasher soap, I can just grab a cute tablet from my blue canning jar on the counter and toss it in the dishwasher.

SQUEEGEE

If you haven't used a squeegee in your cleaning adventures, you need to purchase one. A squeegee truly changed my window-washing life! You can simply spray your solution on the window and squeegee it off. Or you can get a squeegee with a sponge attached to use on especially dirty windows. Simply dip the sponge into a bucket containing window cleaner, scrub the window, and squeegee away the dirt. You'll need a couple of extra towels around your workspace to avoid drips and spills, but it's worth it.

SPONGES

You probably have these on hand, of course! Regular sponges have no odor or cleaner, so they're great for using with the products in this book. For certain jobs, I love melamine sponges—you might have heard of a popular brand name, Magic Eraser. I usually try to clean a stain simply with the sponge and water first, and if that doesn't get the mark or dirt off, I dip the sponge in a little soapy water or squirt a little Lemon and Peppermint All-Purpose Cleaner on the sponge or surface mixed with a little warm water. Never use these sponges on surfaces like high-gloss paint or on any type of countertop; if you are unsure, test in an inconspicuous place first.

DUSTING WANDS

Look for a dusting wand with a washable duster for the most economical choice. A duster with an extendable pole will reach corners and tall ceilings.

BROOM

A broom and dustpan may seem old-fashioned, but for little cleanups and spills, a broom is just the thing.

MOP

Look for a mop that fits your needs. You might like a sponge mop, a twistable mop, or—my preference—a refillable mop with microfiber pads that can be washed in the washing machine.

BUCKETS

Every house needs a bucket (or two or three). I keep one for the toilet plunger, one for soapy mixtures, and one for cleaning rags.

VACUUM CLEANER WITH ATTACHMENTS

Buy the best vacuum cleaner with attachments that you can afford. To me, that money is well spent. Make sure it has a decent warranty and take good care of it by emptying and cleaning the canister or replacing the bag often.

TOILET BRUSH

Toilet brushes are necessary for toilet cleaning. Find one that works and keep it in a discreet place.

FUNNEL

A funnel comes in very handy for recipes where you'll mix a solution, then pour it into a bottle to use and store.

TOOL CONTAINERS OR CADDIES

Corral your cleaners and tools in a tool container or caddy that fits neatly in a closet and holds what you want it to hold. That way, your tools are right where you need them, saving you time and energy when it's time to clean that area. You'll probably find that you want a few caddies in key spots in your home.

LABEL IT!

Adding a label to your cleaning products will ensure that any product saved is used properly. Use a label maker, send labels through the printer, or just place a piece of tape on the container and write your necessary information on the tape with a permanent marker. Use a cute label for gifts or just to boost the design factor of your homemade cleaning products. Make sure that you include the name of the product, the ingredients, and a use-by date. If it's a product that you find yourself mixing up regularly, you can even write the recipe on the bottle, so you can quickly mix it up the next time you need it.

Gather Basic Ingredients

Many natural cleaners use the same base ingredients. You will find that you already have a lot of these ingredients in your home. If not, you can find borax, Arm & Hammer Super Washing Soda, and castile soap at your local big-box store in the laundry and natural beauty sections. If you prefer to order from the comfort of your home, all the items can be found easily on *www.amazon.com* as well.

Store all ingredients in a cool, dry place. Just purchase what you need at first, then decide which cleaners you want to keep on hand based on your particular cleaning needs.

DISTILLED WHITE VINEGAR

Vinegar is the powerhouse in the cleaning cabinet. It has germ-killing properties, cuts grease, and gets rid of stains. It's not my favorite smell (I don't like my house to smell like a pickle), but I have lots of ways to disguise the vinegar odor in my recipes.

WATER—DISTILLED AND TAP

You'll use both distilled and tap water in the recipes. Distilled water has gone through a distillation process that essentially removes contaminants and minerals. This makes it a great candidate for using in cleaning products because you aren't introducing any minerals or bacteria into the mix, which would cut down on the shelf life of the products. If you don't want to buy distilled water, you can boil and cool tap water with similar results.

BAKING SODA

Baking soda works great for absorbing odors and as a mild abrasive cleaner. Look for baking soda in your grocery store's baking aisle, or pick up a big bag at your favorite warehouse store.

SUPER WASHING SODA

Super Washing Soda is a scentless powder sold under the Arm & Hammer brand name. It is simply sodium carbonate and water—basically an amped-up version of baking soda. Super Washing Soda is a detergent booster and odor and stain remover, and can be used in many organic cleaning recipes with great results. If you can't find it at your supermarket, you can order it on Amazon.com.

BORAX

Available in just about every super-market, borax is a naturally occurring mineral found where saltwater lakes and seawater have evaporated. There is some controversy as to its safety if inhaled or in-gested, so take extra care when using this ingredient. Keep it out of the reach of chil-dren and pets, thoroughly rinse all surfac-es you use it on, and (as with all powdery ingredients) avoid inhaling it when mix-ing it in a recipe. That extra care is well worth it because of the results it gives!

CASTILE SOAP—BAR AND LIQUID

I love Dr. Bronner's castile soaps. They are certified organic and can be found at most supermarkets and on Amazon.com. Better yet, they are avail-able in a wide variety of scents as well as unscented. Castile soap is a vegetable-based soap, making it especially gentle, but the combination of vegetable oils like coconut and olive make it extremely effective in cleaning and grease cutting.

ESSENTIAL OILS

Essential oils are the natural oils from plants. (Don't confuse these with fragrance oils, which are not the same.) Super-concentrated, these oils are known for their scent, and some have antibacterial and antifungal properties as well as amazing cleaning abilities (see the next section for more information).

Make sure that any essential oils you purchase are pure, food-grade, and sold in brown or blue glass vials or bottles. You'll want at least one or two essen-tial oils to add to your natural clean-ing products. If I could choose only two oils, I'd pick lemon and tea tree (also found as *Melaleuca*). Lemon has a fresh scent and tea tree has strong disinfect-ing properties. Take care handling the oils and never let children handle them, as they are extremely potent and con-centrated and can cause skin irritation.

LEMONS AND LEMON JUICE

Some people think you can clean your whole house with lemons and vinegar. I think there are a few other ingredients that should come to the cleaning party, but lemons are definitely a must. Lemons and lemon juice have antibacterial prop-erties and are great cleaning agents—and you can't beat their fresh scent!

SALTS—EPSOM AND KOSHER

Epsom salts are not salt, but a com-pound of magnesium and sulfate. Epsom salts can be ingested for ailments, used in bath water to ease muscle soreness, and used to soften water. Epsom salts work well to form cleaning tablets and have some softening properties in natural dish soap. Kosher salt is a great abrasive cleaner. Add a little lemon juice and you have a natural antibacterial scrub.

OILS—ALMOND, OLIVE, VITAMIN E, MINERAL, AND COCONUT

Some popular oils to use in organic cleaning products are almond, olive, vitamin E, mineral, and coconut. You don't need to keep *all* of these oils on hand, but it's nice to have a few. You'll see that most of these oils are used in wood care and in soaps to help condition the skin.

HYDROGEN PEROXIDE

Sold in the pharmacy section for usually under a dollar a bottle, hydrogen peroxide is an all-natural sanitizer and disinfectant. It's so safe that you can disinfect toothbrushes with it. It is unscented and needs to be kept in a dark container (just keep it in the brown container it is sold in). Its scentless and gasless properties are what make hydrogen peroxide a great disinfectant. If you have a cutting board that you just cut up raw chicken on, wash it with soap and water and spray hydrogen peroxide on it to ensure any salmonella has been obliterated. You can also follow the peroxide spray with a spray of white vinegar for super-germy messes (but never mix the two together in one bottle).

ALCOHOL—RUBBING ALCOHOL AND VODKA

Rubbing alcohol (or isopropyl alcohol) is found in the pharmacy section for under a dollar a bottle. It is sold as an antiseptic, and those antiseptic qualities are what give rubbing alcohol its germ-killing properties. You might be surprised to see that I use vodka in a number of recipes in this book. Vodka has a high alcohol content that allows it to kill germs, mold, and mildew. I generally prefer vodka to rubbing alcohol because the scent is less noticeable and it produces similar results.

PURE ALOE VERA GEL

Aloe vera is a succulent plant whose leaves produce a gel-like substance commonly used in cosmetics and body care products for its soothing qualities. Make sure that you choose the pure aloe vera gel and not the green stuff. You can use the leftover gel for burn relief, and I love it in the hand sanitizer recipe.

CREAM OF TARTAR

Found in the baking aisle, this ingredient is great for whitening.

OXYGEN BLEACH POWDER

There is a homemade recipe for oxygen bleach paste in this book, but you can also safely use store-bought oxygen bleach powder in your home. Oxygen bleach powder removes stains and whitens without bleach. The homemade variety of oxygen bleach paste has a very short shelf life, so you may find the store-bought powder to be more conducive to your needs.

Cleaning with Essential Oils

Essential oils actually have cleaning and disinfecting power in addition to smelling great. Following are the essential oils that you'll find used in my recipes. There are many health benefits to using essential oils—but for the purposes of this book, here are each oil's cleaning and disinfecting qualities. You can buy essential oils at your local health food store or at a variety of stores online. Make sure you are purchasing pure essential oils, not fragrance oils. Some of my favorite brands include Beeyoutiful, doTERRA, and Mountain Rose Herbs.

ESSENTIAL OIL USES

ESSENTIAL OIL	USES
Citronella	insect repellent
Clove	air freshener
Eucalyptus	anti-infective, deodorant
Grapefruit	air freshener, antiseptic
Lavender	antifungal, antiseptic, anti-infective
Lemon	antifungal, antiseptic, anti-infective, antiviral
Lime	air freshener
Orange	air freshener
Peppermint	antibacterial, antifungal, antiseptic, antiviral
Rosemary	antibacterial, antifungal, anti-infective, antimicrobial, antiseptic
Tea tree	antibacterial, antifungal, antimicrobial, antiseptic, antiviral

Mixing Guidelines

Now that you have your tools assembled and your basic ingredients on hand, it's time to start making some recipes! Here are a few tips and tricks that apply to all the recipes:

- Take care to make the recipes as directed. Keep ingredients and finished products out of the reach of pets and children.
- You can make these recipes right in your kitchen sink, but if you have a mudroom or laundry room sink, those will work too. If you are working in the kitchen, make sure you don't have any food out while mixing up powders or anything that could travel to your food.
- You can use the same measuring cups, spoons, and scoops that you use for cooking and baking to make these recipes. Everything is nontoxic—a simple run through the dishwasher is all that's necessary for a quick cleanup of the measuring and mixing tools. Isn't that great?
- If you have any leftovers, turn the faucet water on cold and pour down the drain. None of these ingredients will have any ill effects on your drains or septic system.

CHAPTER 3

RECIPES FOR THE KITCHEN

Feel like you spend the bulk of your time in the kitchen? You probably do! As a result, you probably have a lot of cleaning questions: How do I keep the kitchen clean, especially while trying to get dinner on the table in a hurry? What's the best way to sanitize the cutting board after slicing raw poultry? How can I quickly clean my refrigerator and not waste any time doing it? The kitchen poses both potential health hazards and endless cleaning tasks. Figuring out the best way to clean everything from the cupboards to the floors while keeping your family safe from foodborne illnesses seems tricky. With the recipes in this chapter, you know that your counters and other surfaces are not only clean but safely sanitized using organic and natural products. Your kitchen will be clean from top to bottom and you'll know exactly how to pronounce each and every ingredient you used.

Citrus Liquid Hand Soap

8 OUNCES

Store-bought antibacterial soap is proven to get rid of germs, but it also gets rid of the "good germs" that our bodies need to build up immunities. This fresh-smelling blend will eliminate garlic and onion odors from your hands and get your hands perfectly clean and rid of germs without the use of chemicals like triclosan.

1 CUP LIQUID CASTILE SOAP

10 DROPS LEMON ESSENTIAL OIL

10 DROPS ORANGE ESSENTIAL OIL

1 TEASPOON VITAMIN E OIL

Variations:

UNSCENTED — Use unscented castile soap and don't add any essential oils.

PEPPERMINT AND LAVENDER — Substitute 10 drops peppermint and 10 drops lavender essential oils for the lemon and orange.

LEMON AND ROSEMARY — Substitute 10 drops rosemary essential oil for the orange.

To Make: Combine ingredients in a decorative soap pump, seal, and shake thoroughly to combine.

To Use: Use a pump of soap, rub hands together, and wash off with warm water.

To Store: Make this citrusy hand soap one soap pump at a time.

HELPFUL HINT

Recite a nursery rhyme or sing "Happy Birthday" for a full 30 seconds while washing to effectively wash all the germs from your hands.

Citrus Foaming Hand Soap

1 16-OUNCE DISPENSER OR 2 8-OUNCE DISPENSERS

Foaming-soap dispensers are a great way to make your liquid soap last longer. You only need 1 or 2 tablespoons of liquid soap for the whole soap dispenser! This is a great way to stretch out your soap when you have lots of family members washing their hands constantly.

2 CUPS WATER, BOILED AND COOLED
(or distilled, if you won't use all the soap in a week or two)

1–2 TABLESPOONS CASTILE SOAP

10–20 DROPS LEMON OR ORANGE ESSENTIAL OIL

Variations:

UNSCENTED — Use unscented castile soap and don't add any essential oil.

PEPPERMINT AND LAVENDER — Substitute 10 drops peppermint and 10 drops lavender essential oils for the lemon or orange.

EXTRA MOISTURIZING — Add 1 teaspoon vitamin E oil.

To Make: Pour ingredients into pump dispenser. Start with 10 drops of essential oil and add more, to your preference. Shake to combine.

To Use: Dispense 1 or 2 pumps on your hands and scrub away.

To Store: With distilled water: Store in pump for several months. With undistilled water: Store in pump for 2 weeks.

TIME-SAVING TIP

Mix the Citrus Liquid Hand Soap (see recipe earlier in this chapter) first and then fill your foaming-soap dispensers with 2 tablespoons of the liquid soap and 2 cups of water. Shake to combine.

Lemon and Clove Liquid Dish Soap

8 OUNCES

Lemon and clove is my favorite scent combination and it's especially wonderful in the kitchen with a sink full of dishes. It's even better when the dishes are clean, streak-free, and put away, but that's another story.

8 OUNCES CITRUS CASTILE SOAP OR UNSCENTED CASTILE SOAP

10–15 DROPS LEMON ESSENTIAL OIL

5 DROPS CLOVE ESSENTIAL OIL

Variations:

GREASE FIGHTING — Add a splash of white vinegar to the warm dishwater.

CITRUS — Substitute orange, lime, or grapefruit essential oil for the clove.

To Make: Pour castile soap and essential oils in storage container and shake well to combine.

To Use: Add 1 or 2 squirts to your dishwater and scrub up!

To Store: Store indefinitely on your counter or under your sink.

TIME-SAVING TIP

Add essential oils directly to the castile soap container. Label and use often!

Lemon Dishwasher Detergent—Powder

ABOUT 24 LOADS—1 heaping tablespoon per load

It's especially important to avoid using toxic chemicals on things we eat and drink from. Rest assured that with this recipe, all you'll get is sparkly clean dishes. The fresh scent is amazing and it mixes up in a snap.

1 CUP ARM & HAMMER SUPER WASHING SODA

1 CUP BAKING SODA

1 CUP BORAX

20 DROPS LEMON ESSENTIAL OIL

Variations:

FOR HARD WATER—Add ½ cup Epsom salts.

UNSCENTED—Omit the essential oil.

LEMON AND PEPPERMINT—Use 10 drops lemon and 10 drops peppermint essential oils.

CITRUS—Use 10 drops lemon and 10 drops orange essential oils.

To Make: Combine ingredients in a large mixing bowl.

To Use: Place 1 heaping tablespoon per load in the dish detergent compartment and run as usual.

To Store: Pour into a glass container with a lid. (I love antique colored canning jars for dish powder storage. They look stylish and keep the mixture dry.)

HELPFUL HINT

If you have hard water, you know that you have various issues when it comes to spots on your glassware and dishes. The Epsom salts will nontoxically soften the water and will help to eliminate spots on your glassware. If you have already installed a water softener in your home or you don't need a water softener, you may still get spots on glassware if you aren't using a rinsing agent in your dishwasher. You can add white vinegar to your rinse dispenser to act as a rinse aid, and you can try the Epsom salts in your dishwasher detergent recipe. Start with ¼ cup of vinegar instead of the full ½ cup and increase if needed. Feel free to add the Epsom salts in your detergent recipe right along with the vinegar rinse. Experiment to find the perfect ratio for your water.

Lemon Dishwasher Detergent—Liquid

Prefer liquid dishwasher detergent to powdered? Try this simple recipe. You'll love the fresh lemon scent that fills your kitchen while this is working its magic in your dishwasher.

1 CUP CASTILE SOAP

¼ CUP WATER, DISTILLED OR BOILED AND COOLED SLIGHTLY

1 TEASPOON LEMON JUICE

5 DROPS LEMON ESSENTIAL OIL

To Make: Mix ingredients in a bowl and pour into a container that has a lid or spout for easy pouring into your dishwasher's detergent compartment.

To Use: Use 1 tablespoon per load and run as usual.

To Store: Store at room temperature for up to 3 weeks.

HELPFUL HINT

Add distilled white vinegar to the rinse compartment of your dishwasher to remove hard water spots from your glasses and dishware.

Lemon Dishwasher Detergent—Tablets

Cleaning products in tablet form are very popular. If this is your preference, you'll love this cleaning solution for its simple ingredients, great scent, and how well it works to get dishes completely clean and residue-free.

2 CUPS BAKING SODA

2 CUPS BORAX

½ CUP WHITE VINEGAR

20 DROPS LEMON ESSENTIAL OIL

ICE CUBE TRAYS

Variations:

FOR HARD WATER — Add ½ cup Epsom salts.

UNSCENTED — Omit the essential oil.

LEMON AND PEPPERMINT — Use 10 drops lemon and 10 drops peppermint essential oils.

CITRUS — Use 10 drops lemon and 10 drops orange essential oils.

To Make: Combine the dry ingredients in a large mixing bowl. Slowly add the white vinegar and stir to combine. The vinegar will create a fizzing action. Once the mixture is thoroughly combined, measure rounded tablespoons into several ice cube trays and press down to form the tablets. Do not fill the trays to the top, just use a rounded tablespoon in each compartment. Allow to dry out and harden overnight or in the sun. Once the tablets have hardened, carefully turn the tray over onto a clean surface. The tablets should fall out without any twisting or banging, which could break them into pieces.

To Use: Place 1 tablet in the dish detergent compartment and run as usual.

To Store: Store in an airtight glass or plastic container for up to 2 months.

KID-FRIENDLY TIP

This is a fun recipe for little ones to help with once the powders are measured and in the bowl. My kids love to add the vinegar to see the fizzing and they have fun pushing the detergent into the ice cube trays with a tablespoon.

Oven Cleaner—Spray

8 OUNCES

If your oven needs a little cleaning, this is the perfect cleaning solution. It mixes up in a hurry and does a great job removing stuck-on food and grease.

1 CUP WARM WATER

3 TABLESPOONS BAKING SODA

1 TABLESPOON CASTILE SOAP

Variations:

LEMON — Add 10 drops lemon essential oil.

LEMON AND CLOVE — Add 5 drops lemon and 5 drops clove essential oils.

LEMON AND ROSEMARY — Add 5 drops lemon and 5 drops rosemary essential oils.

To Make: Add ingredients to a spray bottle and shake to combine.

To Use: Spray liberally in your oven. Let sit for up to 15 minutes and wipe clean with a sponge or cloth. Rinse as needed and allow to air-dry.

To Store: If you have any leftovers, you can store this solution for up to 2 weeks. Shake to combine, as the ingredients will settle.

TIME-SAVING TIP

If you have extra cleaning solution, spray down your stovetop and clean that area while you're there!

Oven Cleaner—Paste

1 CLEAN OVEN

Spills that go unattended in the bottom of an oven are difficult to remove. With this powerful paste, you'll be able to wipe the grime away in a hurry.

½ CUP WATER

¾—1 CUP BAKING SODA

1 TABLESPOON CASTILE OR DISH SOAP

Variation:

LEMON—Add 1 or 2 squeezes of fresh lemon juice to harness the cleaning power of lemon and to add a fresh scent.

To Make: Combine ingredients in a bowl to form a paste.

To Use: Apply with a sponge, coating the oven. Let sit for 15 to 30 minutes. Using a clean sponge, rinse thoroughly with warm water. Repeat the rinsing with a sponge and warm water until the oven is completely clean.

To Store: This is a one-time-use product; no storage necessary.

Oven Cleaner—Overnight

1 CLEAN OVEN

If it's been a long time since you cleaned your oven, or if your mother-in-law is visiting, this is the oven cleaner for you.

1 CUP WATER

¾–1 CUP BAKING SODA

2 TABLESPOONS CASTILE OR DISH SOAP

To Make: Combine ingredients in a bowl to form a paste.

To Use: Turn oven on to 250°F; let it come to temperature and turn off. Quickly apply the solution with a sponge, coating the oven. Close the door and let it work overnight. The next day, spray thoroughly with warm water. Using a clean sponge, rinse thoroughly with warm water. Repeat the rinsing with a sponge and warm water until the oven is completely clean.

To Store: This is a one-time-use product; no storage necessary.

Filter Cleaner (Stove and Hood)

1 OR 2 CLEAN FILTERS

Did you know that there's probably a washable filter hiding in your range or hood? If you haven't cleaned your filter before, it's time to start! If you have cleaned your filter or regularly clean it, you'll appreciate this easy method.

½ CUP WATER

½ CUP DISTILLED WHITE VINEGAR

1 TEAPOT OF BOILING WATER

To Make: Mix ½ cup water and vinegar in spray bottle.

To Use: Place filter in sink and spray vinegar and water mixture on. Let sit for at least 15 minutes to dissolve grease and grime. Pour boiling water over filter(s) and repeat if necessary.

To Store: This is a one-time-use product; no storage necessary.

TIME-SAVING TIP

Clean all your washable filters (you might also find filters on your oven vent, stovetop, air conditioners, etc.) at the same time. Add this task to your cleaning checklist to be sure you remember them. Depending on how much cooking you do, it's best done monthly or quarterly.

Lemon Microwave Oven Cleaner—Spray

1 CLEAN MICROWAVE

Everyone has accidentally had something spill or explode in the microwave. What a mess! This spray will have the entire thing sparkling again in no time.

¼ CUP WATER

¼ CUP DISTILLED WHITE VINEGAR

¼ CUP LEMON JUICE

To Make: Add ingredients to a spray bottle and shake to combine.

To Use: Spray liberally on interior of microwave. Let sit for 15 minutes to dissolve any dirt and grease. Wipe clean with a sponge or microfiber cloth. Repeat if necessary, rinse, and dry.

To Store: Store in spray bottle for up to 1 week.

Lemon Microwave Oven Cleaner—Steam

1 CLEAN MICROWAVE

Using steam to clean messes and grease off the interior of a microwave is simple but extremely effective. The best perk is the smell from the juice of the fresh lemon while the microwave cleans itself.

4 CUPS WATER
1 LEMON

To Make: Place water in a microwaveable bowl. Cut the lemon in half and juice it. Add the juice *and* the lemon halves to the bowl. Run the microwave until the water boils (3–5 minutes). When done, let the mixture sit and steam in the microwave for 15–30 minutes.

To Use: Remove the bowl and wipe microwave clean with a clean, damp cloth or sponge. Wipe dry.

To Store: This is a one-time-use product; no storage necessary.

TIME-SAVING TIP

This cleaning task is mostly hands-off and can easily be done while you're working on other things in the kitchen.

Cabinet Cleaner

....

Cabinets don't always show their dirt, but believe me, it's there! Once your cabinets are clean, you'll see what a difference a little scrubbing can do. This simple recipe will cut grease and fingerprints and it offers a little aromatherapy to boot. Use it on your cabinet and drawer fronts and insides. This solution works with any finished cabinets—wood, laminate, or veneer. Make sure you squeeze any excess liquid from your cloth to keep unnecessary water off your cabinets.

8 CUPS WARM WATER

2 TEASPOONS CASTILE SOAP

3 DROPS LEMON ESSENTIAL OIL

Variation:

UNSCENTED — Omit the essential oil.

To Make: Mix ingredients in a small bucket.

To Use: Start at the top left side of your cabinets and scrub your way down and to the right with a sponge or microfiber cloth.

To Store: This is a one-time-use product; no storage necessary.

HELPFUL HINT

Use a microfiber cloth on cabinets and drawers—the microfiber will grab little crumbs easily and wipe the fingerprints and smudges away with ease.

Lemon and Peppermint All-Purpose Cleaner

Generally, homemade cleaners are not meant to be mixed up in large quantities because they don't have stabilizers, or artificial ingredients intended to extend the shelf life of the ingredients. It's a good idea to test any homemade cleaner in an inconspicuous spot to make sure that it's safe on the surface you are intending to use it on. A warning: **Don't use any vinegar products on granite or marble.** *The acid in the vinegar will eat away at your granite and marble.*

½ CUP WHITE VINEGAR

JUICE OF 1 LEMON

2 CUPS WATER

10 DROPS PEPPERMINT ESSENTIAL OIL

Variations:

LEMON AND CLOVE — Substitute clove essential oil for the peppermint.

LEMON AND ROSEMARY — Substitute rosemary essential oil for the peppermint.

To Make: Add ingredients to a spray bottle and shake to combine.

To Use: Spray counters, sinks, tables, appliances, and any other kitchen item with this all-purpose cleaner. This cleaner is a powerhouse, cutting through dirt, grime, and grease, and it will clean just about every surface in your kitchen. The lemon and vinegar also have germ-killing properties that you'll love!

To Store: This recipe has fresh lemon juice in it—use it within a few days of making it and/or store in the refrigerator for up to 1 week.

Lemon and Peppermint All-Purpose Cleaning Concentrate

. . . .

32 OUNCES

Create your own cleaning concentrate by adding essential oils to vinegar.

32-OUNCE BOTTLE OF WHITE VINEGAR
30 DROPS LEMON ESSENTIAL OIL
10 DROPS PEPPERMINT ESSENTIAL OIL

To Make: Add essential oils to the 32-ounce bottle of vinegar, seal, and shake to combine.

To Use: Pour ½ cup of the vinegar mixture into a spray bottle. Add 2 cups of water and the juice of a lemon. Spray counters, sinks, tables, appliances, and any other kitchen item with this all-purpose cleaner.

To Store: Store in a cool, dark place for up to 2 months.

HELPFUL HINT

Purchase a 32-ounce bottle of white vinegar. Label it with your concoction and you've got a ready-made storage container!

Tea Tree and Orange Disinfecting Cleaner

....

2 ½ CUPS

Disinfection isn't necessary all the time, but it's good to have an all-natural cleaning solution for those times that you need to disinfect, like when you've just cut up a raw chicken. Enter this recipe—no harmful fumes, just all-natural disinfection from the germ-killing powerhouses vinegar and tea tree. The Super Washing Soda adds a little extra cleaning kick. The boiled water kills germs in the water, giving the cleaner a longer shelf life, and using hot water helps dissolve the ingredients.

½ CUP WHITE VINEGAR

1 TEASPOON ARM & HAMMER SUPER WASHING SODA

20 DROPS TEA TREE ESSENTIAL OIL

10 DROPS ORANGE ESSENTIAL OIL

2 CUPS BOILED AND SLIGHTLY COOLED WATER

To Make: Add ingredients to a spray bottle and shake to combine.

To Use: Spray surfaces, let sit for 10 minutes, and wipe clean with a cleaning cloth or paper towel.

To Store: Store in spray bottle for up to 2 weeks.

Tea Tree and Orange Disinfecting Cleaning Concentrate

32 OUNCES

Making your own cleaning concentrate is simple—just add to a spray bottle with water and you're ready to clean and disinfect!

32-OUNCE BOTTLE OF WHITE VINEGAR

50 DROPS TEA TREE ESSENTIAL OIL

30 DROPS ORANGE ESSENTIAL OIL

Variation:

EXTRA CLEANING POWER — Add 1 teaspoon Super Washing Soda to your water and concentrate.

To Make: Add essential oils to the vinegar, seal, and shake to combine.

To Use: Pour ½ cup of the vinegar mixture into a spray bottle. Add 2 cups of water and shake to combine. Spray counters, sinks, tables, appliances, and any other kitchen item with this disinfecting cleaner. Spray surfaces and let sit for 10 minutes, then wipe clean with a cleaning cloth, sponge, or paper towel.

To Store: Store in a cool, dark place for up to 2 months.

Lemon and Clove Nightly Sink Scrub

2 CUPS

This is one of my favorite homemade cleaning solutions. I keep mine in a vintage blue canning jar under my kitchen sink and use it nightly with a dishwasher-safe scrub brush. Once the dishes are done and the counters are wiped down, I scrub the sink. I put out a clean hand towel and my kitchen is clean and ready for another day.

2 CUPS BAKING SODA

10 DROPS LEMON ESSENTIAL OIL

10 DROPS CLOVE ESSENTIAL OIL

1 SQUIRT OF LEMON AND CLOVE DISH SOAP (see recipe earlier in this chapter)

Variations:

UNSCENTED — Omit the essential oils.

CITRUS — Add 10 drops orange or grapefruit essential oil.

To Make: Add baking soda to a jar or container and scent with essential oils. Stir to combine.

To Use: Wet kitchen sink. Sprinkle a little bit of the baking soda mixture in sink—up to ¼ cup. Add a squirt of dish soap to the mixture and scrub with scrub brush. Rinse and air-dry or dry with a cloth or paper towel.

To Store: Store in a cool, dark place indefinitely.

Fruit and Veggie Wash

12 OUNCES

It's important to wash any pesticides and germs off your produce. This solution removes all those residues and has germ-killing properties to boot.

½ CUP APPLE CIDER VINEGAR

½ CUP LEMON JUICE

½ CUP WATER

To Make: Add ingredients to a spray bottle and shake to combine.

To Use: Spray liberally on fruits and vegetables, then rinse in cold water and prepare as usual.

To Store: Store in the refrigerator for up to 1 month.

GIFT-GIVING TIP

Mix up a spray bottle of this veggie wash, add a cute label, and package it with a peck of local apples for a friend.

Sticker and Goo Remover

ABOUT 1 TABLESPOON

Have a stuck-on label or sticker? Try this paste. It mixes up in a snap and will remove just about any sticker or goo on hard surfaces.

1 TABLESPOON BAKING SODA

1 TABLESPOON ALMOND OR VEGETABLE OIL

Variations:

LEMON — Add 1 or 2 drops of lemon essential oil if you'd like a little scent with your goo removal.

LARGER BATCH — Use ¼ cup baking soda and ¼ cup oil. Combine and store in a glass container in a cool, dark place.

To Make: Combine baking soda and oil in small glass or plastic container.

To Use: Apply a small amount to spot. Let sit for a minute or two to soak. Rub with a paper towel or cleaning cloth to remove. Repeat if necessary. If there's a little oily residue remaining, apply rubbing alcohol to a cotton ball and wipe to remove any residue.

To Store: Store in a sealed container for up to 1 month.

GIFT-GIVING TIP

Mix up a double batch of this paste and put half in a cute jar with a label and give to a friend that is moving or has just moved. This all-natural cleaning solution will be perfect for all the stickers that need to be removed when moving into a new home!

Stainless Steel Cleaner

AS MUCH AS NEEDED

Cleaning stainless steel has left me in a conundrum. There are so many commercial cleaners out there, but none of them work on all my appliances, and who wants to buy multiple stainless steel cleaners? This simple solution may surprise you, but all you need is a little vinegar and microfiber to clean your stainless steel. Don't believe me? Give it a try—it's amazing!

DISTILLED WHITE VINEGAR

To Make: Pour or spray a little vinegar directly on a microfiber cleaning cloth—not on your stainless steel. If possible, use a cloth designed for stainless steel or windows and mirrors.

To Use: Apply to your appliances going with the grain of your stainless steel and from top to bottom. Buff as needed.

To Store: Keep your vinegar and cleaning cloth handy to quickly wipe fingerprints and smudges on your appliances when needed.

TIME-SAVING TIP

Stuck on hold during a phone call? That's a great time to accomplish small cleaning tasks like this one!

Stainless Steel Polish

....

AS MUCH AS NEEDED

If your stainless steel needs a little shine after you've cleaned it, you need a little oil. The oil will protect the stainless steel and prevent smudges. Polishing stainless steel isn't a necessity but it does make a difference. Try this easy technique after you've cleaned your appliances.

ALMOND OIL

To Make: Pour a small amount of the almond oil on your cloth.

To Use: Using your cloth with the almond oil, buff your stainless steel in the direction of the grain and from top to bottom. Use a separate cloth to buff off any excess.

To Store: Keep your almond oil in your kitchen so it's handy for polishing.

Refrigerator Cleaner

....

1 CLEAN AND DEODORIZED REFRIGERATOR

A clean refrigerator is nice to look at, but keeping it clean can also save you money, since you'll be accessing forgotten food that's stashed in the back. This cleaning process is most easily done when you have an almost empty refrigerator.

2 GALLONS WARM WATER

2 TABLESPOONS CASTILE SOAP OR DISH SOAP

2 TABLESPOONS BAKING SODA

TIME-SAVING TIP

Do a quick refrigerator cleanout when you make your weekly grocery list. Wipe up any spills, toss old food, and make room for fresh groceries. Doing this weekly keeps the refrigerator clean (or at least cleaner) from week to week.

To Make: Mix 1 gallon warm water, 1 tablespoon castile soap or dish soap, and 1 tablespoon baking soda in a large container or bucket until dissolved. Then, fill your sink with water (about 1 gallon) and add 1 tablespoon castile soap or dish soap and 1 tablespoon baking soda to wash the drawers and shelves.

To Use: Empty refrigerator of food contents (place items in a cooler with ice if you anticipate this taking more than 15 minutes). Place shelves and drawers in sink to soak. Using a microfiber cloth or clean washcloth, wipe down your refrigerator from top to bottom, rinsing and wringing out your cleaning cloth as needed. Once refrigerator has been thoroughly wiped clean, dry with a clean dish towel and head to your sink. Wash, rinse, and dry shelves and drawers. Return the shelves and drawers back to your refrigerator along with the food. Place a box of baking soda in your refrigerator to absorb any lingering odors.

To Store: This is a one-time-use product; no storage necessary.

Freezer Cleaner

....

1 CLEAN AND DEODORIZED FREEZER

Cleaning your freezer can be difficult because adding water to a freezer just creates ice. This simple recipe and solution will help you clean your freezer quickly and get you back to more important things.

2 CUPS WARM WATER

¼ CUP BAKING SODA

To Make: Mix ingredients in a bowl until dissolved.

To Use: Empty freezer of its contents (place items in a cooler with ice if you anticipate this taking more than 15 minutes). Dip a clean cloth in the solution and wring out excess liquid. Starting at the top of the freezer, wipe clean. Soak and clean shelves and drawers with the Refrigerator Cleaner recipe (this chapter), if desired. Return the shelves and drawers back to your freezer along with the food. Place a box of baking soda in your freezer to absorb any lingering odors.

To Store: This is a one-time-use product; no storage necessary.

TIME-SAVING TIP

Combine cleaning your refrigerator and freezer to save time. Make sure you have coolers ready and plenty of cloths and towels to clean and dry all the components.

Laminate Countertop Deep Cleaner

1 KITCHENFUL OF CLEAN COUNTERTOPS

For everyday cleaning of your laminate countertops, use the Lemon and Peppermint All-Purpose Cleaner spray (see recipe earlier in this chapter). If your laminate is looking a little lackluster, give this recipe a try. It's perfect for the times when you really want to clean your countertops thoroughly.

32 OUNCES VERY WARM WATER

3 TABLESPOONS CASTILE SOAP

2 DROPS LEMON ESSENTIAL OIL

Variation:

UNSCENTED — Use unscented castile soap and don't add any essential oil.

To Make: Mix ingredients in container—a plastic storage container or bucket works well.

To Use: Clear all countertops of small appliances and décor. Using a cleaning cloth or microfiber cloth, dip in solution and wipe from the back of the counters to the front, working your way around the kitchen, wiping thoroughly. Rinse cloth often and repeat process with clear water to rinse.

To Store: This is a one-time-use product; no storage necessary.

HELPFUL HINT

Never use an abrasive cleaner on your laminate countertops, because they scratch easily.

Marble Cleaner

16 OUNCES

You should never use vinegar on marble or granite, so what can you clean it with? Soap and water, of course! Here's a super-simple recipe you'll love to use on your marble countertops.

16 OUNCES DISTILLED OR BOILED AND COOLED WATER

1 TEASPOON CASTILE SOAP

To Make: Add ingredients to a spray bottle and shake to combine.

To Use: Spray on marble countertops, wipe with a damp microfiber cloth or sponge. Dry if necessary.

To Store: Store in spray bottle for 1 to 2 months.

HELPFUL HINT

Clean your marble in small, 3' sections to prevent any standing water or spray cleaner sitting on your countertops.

Granite Cleaner

Granite needs extra love and attention when it comes to cleaning. You can clean with warm water and dish soap, but if you'd like a pH-neutral spray that's safe to use on your sealed granite, here's your recipe.

3 TABLESPOONS RUBBING ALCOHOL

2 CUPS WATER

¼ TEASPOON CASTILE SOAP OR DISH SOAP

To Make: Add ingredients to a spray bottle and shake to combine.

To Use: Spray on granite and wipe clean with a microfiber cloth.

To Store: Store in spray bottle for up to 1 month. May separate; just shake before using.

MONEY-SAVING TIP

This solution costs pennies per use, which is much less expensive than commercial granite cleaners, and it is all-natural and safe to use around your family. You'll love how the alcohol speeds the drying process and keeps your counters streak-free. Never let water stand on your granite countertops, as it will stain. Spray and wipe immediately.

Hood/Range Cleaner (Oil-Based)

. . . .

1 CLEAN AND OIL-REPELLENT HOOD AND RANGE

Oil splatters in the kitchen are common, but what's the best way to clean them off a stove hood and oven range? With oil!

VEGETABLE OIL, ALMOND OIL, OR MINERAL OIL

To Make: Apply oil directly to a microfiber cleaning cloth.

To Use: Wipe oiled cloth in the direction of the grain, from top to bottom and left to right.

To Store: This is a one-time-use product; no storage necessary.

TIME-SAVING TIP

If your stove knobs need a little shining up, give them a swipe while you're at it. Wipe the oil on and rub it off for a little natural oil repellent.

Citrus Stove Cleaner

The stove is the powerhouse in the kitchen, so it tends to need frequent cleaning. Try this strong and nontoxic stove cleaner the next time a pot boils over. This simple solution can also be used on a flat electric stovetop.

8 OUNCES HOT WATER

2 TABLESPOONS CASTILE SOAP

2 TABLESPOONS BAKING SODA

5 DROPS LEMON ESSENTIAL OIL

2 DROPS ORANGE ESSENTIAL OIL

Variation:

UNSCENTED — Use unscented castile soap and don't add any essential oils.

To Make: Add ingredients to a spray bottle and shake to combine.

To Use: Spray liberally on stove to cover. Let stand for 15 to 30 minutes. Spray again and wipe clean. Rinse any residue and dry with a clean, dry cloth or paper towels. Microfiber cloths will give you a streak-free shine if you have a flat stovetop.

To Store: Store in spray bottle for up to 1 week.

Kitchen Disinfecting Paste

....

ABOUT ¼ CUP

Icky stuff in your sink, or on your laminate countertop or kitchen workspace? Try this disinfecting paste to kill the germs and give your sink a good scrub at the same time.

½ CUP BAKING SODA

¼ CUP DISTILLED WHITE VINEGAR

10 DROPS TEA TREE ESSENTIAL OIL

To Make: Stir baking soda and vinegar so it forms a paste. Add essential oil and stir to combine—there will be a little fizzing; this is normal.

To Use: Apply to area that needs disinfecting, scrub, and rinse with water. You may need to repeat to completely eliminate stubborn residue.

To Store: This is a one-time-use product; no storage necessary.

TIME-SAVING TIP

If you are disinfecting your sink, mix in sink in lieu of making a paste. Scrub and rinse as directed.

Kitchen Disinfecting Spray

16 OUNCES

This spray can be stored under your kitchen sink and used daily for disinfection. The trick is to let the spray sit for 10 minutes to thoroughly disinfect counters, sinks, and cutting boards. Be careful not to spray on any fabrics, as the hydrogen peroxide has bleaching properties. It is safe for all types of countertops, though.

16-OUNCE CONTAINER OF HYDROGEN PEROXIDE—use the 3 percent solution that you find in a drugstore

SPRAY TOP

To Make: Find a spray top that will fit. Most are universal, so you can wash and reuse a store-bought cleaner's spray top for this purpose. If the tube is too long but the top fits, trim the tube with a pair of scissors. Place spray top on bottle of hydrogen peroxide.

To Use: Rinse any food particles away if you are disinfecting a cutting board or other surface. Spray surface thoroughly with the hydrogen peroxide. Let stand for 10 minutes and wipe or rinse clean. For even stronger sanitation, add castile soap to a sponge and use that to wash and wipe up the solution. Rinse thoroughly and wash as usual.

To Store: Hydrogen peroxide must be stored in a dark container to keep its disinfecting properties, so keep it in its original container.

Small Appliance Cleaner

....

1 KITCHEN FULL OF CLEAN SMALL APPLIANCES

Small appliances don't get the cleaning attention they deserve! You're too busy using the toaster, coffeemaker, and blender to clean them, after all. Give them a little cleaning love with this oh-so-simple technique.

¼ CUP WHITE VINEGAR

5 DROPS ESSENTIAL OIL

To Make: Pour white vinegar in a small bowl and add 5 drops of your favorite essential oil. Lemon is great for this recipe!

To Use: Pour a little vinegar and essential oil mixture onto a damp cleaning cloth. Wipe your small appliances from top to bottom. (You shouldn't even need to rinse and repeat.) The vinegar will dissolve any water spots, grease, and stains.

To Store: Store in an airtight container for up to 2 months.

Lemon Disposal Freshener

....

16 1-OUNCE CUBES

Running your garbage disposal with an ice cube or two helps sharpen the blades a bit. If you use vinegar ice cubes with lemon peel, you have a great freshener.

16 OUNCES WHITE VINEGAR

THE PEEL OF 1 LEMON, COARSELY GRATED

ICE CUBE TRAY(S)

To Make: Pour 16 ounces of white vinegar into a glass measuring cup (this will keep spills to a minimum). Pour vinegar into the ice cube trays and place lemon peel in the white vinegar in each cube spot. Freeze.

To Use: Run cold water in your sink and turn on your disposal. Carefully drop 1 or 2 cubes in disposal and allow to run. Turn off disposal and repeat if necessary.

To Store: Place tray in the freezer overnight. Turn vinegar cubes out into a large zip-top bag and store in the freezer to use when needed.

HELPFUL HINT

If you have an extra lemon or two, grate the peel and place in the freezer for recipes like this one.

Lemon Disposal Cleaner

1 CLEAN AND FRESH DISPOSAL

Is your disposal suffering from stuck-on foods? This weekly cleaner will not only make your kitchen smell great, it'll make your disposal clean and odor-free.

¼ CUP LEMON JUICE

¼ CUP BAKING SODA

To Make: Mix lemon juice and baking soda together to make a pasty liquid.

To Use: Pour mixture down disposal. Let sit for 5 minutes. Run cold water and turn on the disposal and run for a minute or so.

To Store: This is a one-time-use product; no storage necessary.

MONEY-SAVING TIP

Look for large bottles of lemon juice at your favorite warehouse club. You'll have lemon juice on hand for all-natural recipes and you'll save money by buying in bulk.

Lemon Disposal Tablets

....

Prefer a handy tablet for your disposal cleaning and freshening? In addition to freshening your disposal, this simple recipe will give your disposal blades a little workout.

1 CUP BAKING SODA

2–3 TABLESPOONS LEMON JUICE

10 DROPS LEMON ESSENTIAL OIL

ICE CUBE TRAY

To Make: Combine baking soda and lemon juice. Stir to combine—a little fizzing is normal (and fun). Mixture should be dry but packable. Stir in essential oil. Place by the tablespoon into the compartments of an ice cube tray. Allow to dry out and harden overnight or in the sun. Once the tablets have hardened, carefully turn the tray over onto a clean surface. The tablets should fall out without any twisting or banging, which could break them into pieces.

To Use: Run cold water in your sink and drop a tablet in the disposal. Turn off the water and let the tablet sit in the disposal for about 5 minutes to soften a bit. Run disposal as usual.

To Store: Store in an airtight glass or plastic container for up to 1 month.

Natural Drain Unclogger

1 UNCLOGGED DRAIN

Clogged or slow drain got you down? Start your teakettle! If you're unclogging a disposal, add lemon peel to freshen and sharpen the blades a bit.

¼–½ CUP BAKING SODA

¼–½ CUP DISTILLED WHITE VINEGAR

3 DROPS LEMON OR ORANGE ESSENTIAL OIL

3–4 THINLY SLICED CURLICUES FROM A LEMON PEEL (if you are unclogging a disposal)

1 KETTLEFUL OF BOILING WATER

Variation:

UNSCENTED — Omit the essential oil and lemon peel.

To Make: Put 3 drops essential oil directly down the drain to add a nice scent. Add the lemon curlicues and sprinkle baking soda down drain and finish by pouring in distilled white vinegar. Allow to sit for 5–15 minutes.

To Use: Pour hot water down the drain once the solution has done its magic. Then run cold water to see if drain has been cleared. Repeat if necessary.

To Store: This is a one-time-use product; no storage necessary.

TIME-SAVING TIP

While you're waiting for the drain to clear, clean the rest of your kitchen counters. Once you've cleaned them, the drain should be unclogged.

Knife Block Cleaner

1 CLEAN KNIFE BLOCK

This recipe is for those days when you're in cleaning mode and scrubbing everything in sight. Work quickly to prevent any warping of your knife block.

WARM WATER

1 TEASPOON CASTILE SOAP

To Make: Fill your sink with warm water and 1 teaspoon of castile soap or Lemon and Clove Liquid Dish Soap (see recipes earlier in this chapter).

To Use: Dip the knife block in the soapy solution and scrub the holes with a bottle brush. Rinse thoroughly and allow to air-dry, preferably outside in the sun.

To Store: This is a one-time-use product; no storage necessary.

Keurig Cleaner

....

1 CLEAN KEURIG

If that first cup of coffee is a necessary day-starter for you and the Keurig machine is your coffee brewer of choice, you need this recipe. You may not even have realized that it needs to be cleaned to run properly and to last! Don't worry, the process is simple and you probably have all the ingredients on hand.

WHITE VINEGAR

CASTILE OR DISH SOAP

WATER

To Make: Wet a cloth with the vinegar. Fill the kitchen sink with warm water and a few drops of castile or dish soap.

To Use:

• To clean the drip tray and K-cup holder: Remove the drip tray and K-cup holder. If your model has a reservoir, remove that as well. Place these in your sink to soak.

• To clean exterior of machine: If you have water spots on the exterior of the machine, wipe with a little white vinegar on your cleaning cloth. Use a cleaning-designated toothbrush to scrub any small pieces and remove any mineral deposits. Rinse and dry the parts and reassemble your machine.

• To clean the inside of your Keurig: Either fill the reservoir about halfway full with vinegar or, if you don't have a reservoir, place about 10 ounces of vinegar into the water chamber. Run the machine as you normally would, but leave out the K-cup. Repeat once or twice depending on how much mineral buildup is in your machine. Run 2 or 3 cycles with cold water or until there isn't any vinegar smell.

To Store: No storage is necessary, but you may want to keep a toothbrush and vinegar in your kitchen for little cleaning tasks like this.

Coffeepot Cleaner

....

1 CLEAN COFFEEPOT

If washing your coffeepot doesn't usually make the rotation in your cleaning schedule, here's a simple method to clean yours in a hurry. The benefit? Your coffee will taste better and brew more quickly. How's that for motivation?

WATER

WHITE VINEGAR

To Make: Fill coffeepot with equal parts cold water and vinegar.

To Use: Pour solution in the water dispenser and run coffeemaker as usual. Empty solution in sink. Run your coffeepot as usual with 2–3 cycles of cold water or until vinegar smell is gone and water runs clear.

To Store: No storage is necessary, but vinegar and appliances are great friends—keep some vinegar handy!

HELPFUL HINT

Vinegar is a great water spot remover. While you're waiting for the coffee to cycle, pour a little vinegar on a cleaning cloth and wipe away water spots on the coffee machine itself.

Ice Machine Cleaner

Cleaning your refrigerator's icemaker is probably not even on your radar. It should be— it's a hiding spot for bacteria. Not to worry, a clean ice machine is an easy process!

16 OUNCES WARM WATER

CASTILE OR DISH SOAP

To Make: Combine warm water and 1 or 2 drops of soap in a bowl.

To Use: Locate the ice machine in your freezer and carefully remove the ice bin and dump the ice in your kitchen sink. (If you cannot determine how to remove the ice container, consult your owner's manual.) Thoroughly wash and dry. Wipe down entire interior of icemaker with water and soap mixture. Rewipe with a clean wet cloth and dry. Put ice container back and get ready to enjoy clean ice!

To Store: This is a one-time-use product; no storage necessary.

TIME-SAVING TIP

Add this easy step to your refrigerator and freezer cleaning schedule and you'll never forget to clean the ice machine again.

Plastic Storage Container Cleaner

CLEAN PLASTIC STORAGE CONTAINERS

If you use plastic to store leftovers, you've probably experienced a tomato stain or greasy food residue that remains long you've "cleaned" the container. This solution is for those occasions when a stain remains after normal washing.

BAKING SODA

1 TABLESPOON HYDROGEN PEROXIDE

WARM WATER

LIQUID CASTILE SOAP

To Make: Thoroughly rinse the plastic container(s) in warm water. Add hydrogen peroxide to the bottom of your container. Place the cover back on the container and swirl the hydrogen peroxide up the sides of the container if the stain extends up the sides.

To Use: Let container sit with hydrogen peroxide for about an hour. Before dumping the hydrogen peroxide, check to see if the stain is gone. If it isn't gone, sprinkle a little baking soda on top of the hydrogen peroxide and scrub. Wash thoroughly with warm water and castile soap or in your dishwasher. Dry and admire your like-new plastic storage container.

To Store: This is a one-time-use product; no storage necessary.

Teakettle Mineral Deposit Cleaner

1 CLEAN TEAKETTLE

If you're a tea drinker and have hard water, you most likely have mineral deposits in your teakettle. These deposits aren't harmful, but it's easy to remove them.

1 CUP WATER

1 CUP DISTILLED WHITE VINEGAR

To Make: Pour water and vinegar in teakettle. Place the top on the teakettle and put the kettle on the stove and bring to a full boil.

To Use: Allow the water and vinegar mixture to sit in the covered teakettle for at least an hour or overnight. Pour down the drain and wash interior with dish soap. Repeat if necessary. Wipe dry.

To Store: This is a one-time-use product; no storage necessary.

Chemical-Free Silver Cleaner

1 SET OF SPARKLING CLEAN SILVER

The secret to clean silver? Aluminum foil! It's hard to believe that this actually works, but it does a pretty amazing job. The best part? There are no harmful chemicals coming in contact with you or your family.

BAKING SODA—enough to cover the silver, generally about ¼–½ cup

ALUMINUM PAN

ALUMINUM FOIL

1 KETTLEFUL OF BOILING WATER

To Make: Line an aluminum pan (the disposable ones work great) with aluminum foil. Place your silver in the pan.

To Use: Place the pan in a safe place like your kitchen sink or utility sink. Sprinkle baking soda over all your silver. Slowly pour boiling water over the silver. Watch the tarnish disappear. Once the silver is clean—about 15 minutes—wash in soapy water and buff with a soft microfiber or cleaning cloth.

To Store: This is a one-time-use product; no storage necessary.

HELPFUL HINT

Make sure that you keep an eye on the tarnish removal process and handle the silver carefully, as it will be extremely hot.

Disinfecting Wood Cutting Board Cleaner

....

1–2 DISINFECTED CUTTING BOARDS

Cutting boards are great tools in the kitchen, but they need a little care to disinfect them between uses. This simple recipe removes any food residue, and you can rest assured that your cutting boards are clean and ready for their next cooking adventure.

1 LEMON

1–2 TABLESPOONS SALT

To Make: Cut a lemon in half and sprinkle salt on the cut half.

To Use: Rub the lemon half and salt directly on the cutting board to kill germs. Rinse and wash as usual.

To Store: This is a one-time-use product; no storage necessary.

TIME-SAVING TIP

For acrylic and plastic cutting boards, just use a Lemon Dishwasher Detergent Tablet (see recipe earlier in this chapter) and toss them in the dishwasher. Easy peasy!

Lemon and Peppermint Garbage Can Freshening Tablets

16 TABLETS

Place 1 or 2 of these odor-absorbing tablets in the bottom of your garbage can to absorb and eliminate odors.

2 CUPS BAKING SODA

1 CUP EPSOM SALTS OR KOSHER SALT

¼ CUP WATER

10 DROPS LEMON ESSENTIAL OIL

5 DROPS PEPPERMINT ESSENTIAL OIL

ICE CUBE TRAY(S)

Variation:

UNSCENTED — Omit the essential oils.

To Make: Combine the dry ingredients in a large mixing bowl. Slowly add the water and stir to combine. Once the mixture is thoroughly combined, measure rounded tablespoons into the ice cube trays and press down to form the tablets. Do not fill the trays to the top, just use a rounded tablespoon in each compartment. Allow to dry out and harden overnight or in the sun. Once the tablets have hardened, carefully turn the tray over onto a clean surface. The tablets should fall out without any twisting or banging, which could break them into pieces.

To Use: Place 1 or 2 tablets in the bottom of a garbage can to freshen. Replace when you no longer smell the lemon and peppermint.

To Store: Store in an airtight glass or plastic container for 3 months.

CHAPTER 4

RECIPES FOR BATHROOMS

Cleaning bathrooms can be daunting, and it's a chore that definitely doesn't rank high on anyone's list of fun things to do. I thoroughly clean all of the bathrooms in my home on Mondays, sheerly to get it over with! Toxic cleaning products make the situation even worse. Using your own concoctions might change your mind about cleaning your bathroom. You might not rank it at the top of your list, but at least you won't have to wear a mask to get rid of soap scum in your shower! I have formulated some amazing all-natural and organic bathroom cleaning products that you can use on everything from dingy grout, soap-scummed tile, sticky surfaces, toothpaste-splattered mirrors, and stained toilets.

Lavender and Lemon Bathroom Disinfecting Spray

2½ CUPS

Disinfection in the bathroom is a good idea—send white vinegar and vodka, germ-killers extraordinaire, to do the job! You'll keep the harmful fumes away and kill icky germs at the same time.

½ CUP WHITE VINEGAR

½ CUP VODKA

10 DROPS LAVENDER ESSENTIAL OIL

10 DROPS LEMON ESSENTIAL OIL

1½ CUPS BOILED AND SLIGHTLY COOLED WATER

To Make: Add ingredients to a spray bottle and shake to combine. (Use boiled water to dissolve the ingredients properly and kill germs in the water, giving the cleaner a longer shelf life.)

To Use: Spray surfaces, let sit for 10 minutes, and wipe clean with a cleaning cloth or paper towel.

To Store: Store for 1–2 months in a cool, dark place.

Peppermint Daily Shower Cleaner Spray

12 OUNCES

You've cleaned your soap scum from your bathtub and shower and you never want to do it again. How about a daily shower cleaner spray to keep the soap scum at bay?

½ CUP VODKA

1 CUP WATER, DISTILLED OR BOILED AND COOLED

10 DROPS PEPPERMINT ESSENTIAL OIL

Variations:

UNSCENTED — Omit the essential oil.

VINEGAR — No vodka? Just substitute distilled white vinegar for similar results.

To Make: Add ingredients to a spray bottle and shake to combine.

To Use: Spray shower and/or tub daily after all bathing has occurred. No need to rinse; just spray and walk away.

To Store: Store in your shower for 1–2 months.

HELPFUL HINT

Keep a shower squeegee in your shower to help keep the soap scum away—spray daily shower cleaner and squeegee from top to bottom.

Soap Scum Sponges

Make your own soap scum sponges with melamine sponges purchased in bulk. The easiest place to find them is on Amazon.com. You can purchase the melamine precut in various sizes, but you can also cut them to a smaller size for your cleaning project. Just add a little water and the melamine material is transformed into a cleaning powerhouse ready for just about any cleaning endeavor. While the uses are endless, these simple melamine sponges are amazing at removing soap scum and a variety of residues when activated with a little water. Using essential oils will add a little scent to your cleaning project and will also help to remove any residue.

MELAMINE SPONGE

1–2 DROPS OF YOUR FAVORITE ESSENTIAL OIL

To Make: Trim down melamine foam to the desired size with a pair of scissors or a razor blade.

To Use: Add a little water to your sponge, wring out excess water. Add your favorite essential oil and start scrubbing. The sponges are disposable and will eventually disintegrate after about 1–2 uses.

To Store: Store indefinitely.

Soap Scum Remover

Soap scum—is there any way to avoid it? Not really, but you can reduce it: Using castile soap as your shower gel will cut down on soap residue. If you want to get rid of soap scum quickly, two ingredients can banish it in a hurry: borax and water. Get ready to wash your soap scum away!

¼–½ CUP BORAX

2 CUPS HOT WATER

To Make: Add ingredients to a spray bottle and shake to combine.

To Use: Spray thoroughly and let sit for up to 15 minutes. Wipe with a soap scum–removing sponge (melamine). Rinse and wipe dry.

To Store: If you have any mixture left over, find another tub or shower to clean. This is meant to be used up in one cleaning session.

HELPFUL HINT

If you have an extra lemon or two, use them for soap scum removal. Simply cut in half and rub the fruit side of the lemon over the scummy areas. Rinse and repeat if necessary until soap scum is gone.

Lemon and Clove Liquid Hand Soap

8 OUNCES

A moisturizing hand soap is great for the bathroom—this recipe will fill the space with a warm, fresh scent and get your hands squeaky clean.

1 CUP LIQUID CASTILE SOAP

10 DROPS LEMON ESSENTIAL OIL

10 DROPS CLOVE ESSENTIAL OIL

1 TEASPOON VITAMIN E OIL

Variations:

UNSCENTED — Use unscented castile soap and don't add any essential oils.

PEPPERMINT AND LAVENDER — Substitute 10 drops peppermint and 10 drops lavender essential oils for the lemon and clove.

LEMON — Use 20 drops lemon essential oil and no clove.

To Make: Combine ingredients in a soap pump, seal, and shake thoroughly to combine.

To Use: Use a pump of soap, rub hands together, and rinse with warm water.

To Store: Store in pump for several months (if it lasts that long!).

Lemon and Clove Foaming Hand Soap

1 16-OUNCE DISPENSER OR 2 8-OUNCE DISPENSERS

Foaming-soap dispensers are a great way to make your liquid soap last longer. You only need 1–2 tablespoons of liquid soap for the whole soap dispenser, which is very cost-effective when you have a lot of family members washing their hands frequently.

2 CUPS WATER, BOILED AND COOLED
(or distilled water, if you won't use the soap in a week or two)

1–2 TABLESPOONS CASTILE SOAP

10 DROPS LEMON ESSENTIAL OIL

10 DROPS CLOVE ESSENTIAL OIL

Variations:

UNSCENTED — Use unscented castile soap and don't add any essential oils.

PEPPERMINT AND LAVENDER — Substitute 10 drops peppermint and 10 drops lavender essential oils for the lemon and clove.

EXTRA MOISTURIZING — Add 1 teaspoon vitamin E oil to the mixture.

To Make: Pour ingredients into pump dispenser and shake to combine.

To Use: Dispense 1 or 2 pumps on your hands, rub, and scrub away germs.

To Store: With distilled water: Store in pump for several months. With undistilled water: Store in pump for 2 weeks.

TIME-SAVING TIP

First make the Lemon and Clove Liquid Hand Soap (see previous recipe) and then fill up your 8-ounce foaming-soap dispenser with 2 tablespoons of the liquid soap and 2 cups of water.

Lavender and Lemon Disinfecting Cleaning Wipes

24 WIPES

Love the convenience of a wipe but want to know what's in them? Here's a great recipe—that's right, you can even make your own wipes! The white vinegar and vodka help wipe away those germs.

12 THICK AND DURABLE PAPER TOWELS
(such as Bounty DuraTowels)

¼ CUP WHITE VINEGAR

¼ CUP VODKA

5 DROPS LAVENDER ESSENTIAL OIL

5 DROPS LEMON ESSENTIAL OIL

1 CUP BOILED AND SLIGHTLY COOLED WATER

Variation:

UNSCENTED — Omit the essential oils.

To Make: Tear off about a dozen paper towels, cut them in half, and stack into a neat pile. Roll up the stack and stuff them in a 2-cup, wide-mouth mason jar. Mix the ingredients in a large measuring cup and pour over the paper towels in the mason jar. Put the lid on and shake and swirl the liquid around to make sure that it is absorbed into the paper towels. (A large zip-top bag or baby wipe container also works for storing these wipes if you don't have a mason jar—the bag will save space as well.)

To Use: Carefully remove a wipe or two, and use as you would any cleaning wipe.

To Store: Store in a sealed, airtight container for up to 1 week.

TIME-SAVING TIP

Keep cleaning wipes on hand for a quick daily wipe-down of counters and surfaces. A little bit every day will make your weekly cleaning much easier!

Peppermint Window and Mirror Cleaner

16 OUNCES

Everyone notices a dirty window. Use this simple concoction to leave a peppermint scent behind as you clean your windows and mirrors.

2 CUPS WATER, DISTILLED OR BOILED AND COOLED

2 TABLESPOONS DISTILLED WHITE VINEGAR

2 TABLESPOONS RUBBING ALCOHOL

5 DROPS PEPPERMINT ESSENTIAL OIL

To Make: Add ingredients to a spray bottle and shake to combine.

To Use: Spray windows and mirrors, wipe, and admire.

To Store: Store in a cool place for 1–2 months.

HELPFUL HINT

Use a microfiber cloth specifically designed for windows and mirrors. The fibers will glide right along the shiny surface and give you clean and streak-free mirrors and windows in a snap!

Lemon Grout Cleaner

1 TUB OR SHOWER AREA'S WORTH OF CLEAN GROUT

Grimy grout got you down? Try this two-ingredient solution to get rid of it. The cream of tartar and lemon combination will help remove any grout stains and works especially well on colored grout.

2 TEASPOONS CREAM OF TARTAR

LEMON JUICE

To Make: Combine cream of tartar and lemon juice to make a thin paste.

To Use: Apply to grout and scrub with a small cleaning brush. Rinse and wipe dry.

To Store: This is a one-time-use product; no storage necessary.

Lemon Whitening Grout Cleaner

This recipe will breathe new life into your discolored white or light-colored grout!

¼– ½ CUP BAKING SODA

HYDROGEN PEROXIDE

JUICE FROM HALF A LEMON

To Make: In a small container or bowl, mix baking soda and hydrogen peroxide to form a thick paste (fizzing is normal). Stir in the lemon juice to thin the paste or to your desired consistency.

To Use: Test in an inconspicuous place first to make sure that the solution whitens the way you are hoping it will. Wet your small cleaning brush with water and apply the grout cleaner to your grout. Scrub, rinse, and move on!

To Store: This is a one-time-use product; no storage necessary.

Lemon and Peppermint Tile Cleaner

ABOUT 16 OUNCES

If your bathroom has a lot of tile, this will become your go-to bathroom cleaner. It shines tile, removes water spots, and really cleans!

½ CUP WATER

1 TABLESPOON BAKING SODA

¼ CUP WHITE VINEGAR

1 CUP WARM WATER

5 DROPS LEMON ESSENTIAL OIL

3 DROPS PEPPERMINT ESSENTIAL OIL

Variation:

UNSCENTED — Omit the essential oils.

To Make: Add ingredients to a spray bottle and shake to combine.

To Use: Spray thoroughly on tiles. Allow to sit for 5–15 minutes, scrub if necessary, rinse, and dry with a clean cloth or air-dry.

To Store: Store in spray bottle for up to 2 weeks.

Showerhead Cleaner

1 CLEAN SHOWERHEAD

Minerals and soap scum deposit themselves on the showerhead, and over time this build-up minimizes the water pressure and effectiveness of your showerhead. White vinegar can single-handedly take care of this cleaning task—just add a little time and a plastic bag and your showerhead will be like new.

ABOUT A CUP OF DISTILLED WHITE VINEGAR

1 RUBBER BAND

To Make: Pour a cup of vinegar into the plastic bag and lift it to the showerhead. Submerge the spray holes in the vinegar. Add more vinegar if necessary to submerge, and secure the bag to the showerhead with the rubber band.

To Use: Keep the bag on the showerhead for at least 3 hours or overnight. Then remove the bag, rinse, and enjoy the increased water pressure resulting from this minor effort.

To Store: This is a one-time-use product; no storage necessary.

Disinfecting Toilet Bowl Cleaner

1 CLEAN AND DISINFECTED TOILET

Cleaning a toilet is everyone's least favorite cleaning task, but this simple recipe makes it easy.

½ CUP BAKING SODA

¼ CUP WHITE VINEGAR

10 DROPS TEA TREE ESSENTIAL OIL

To Make: Combine ingredients in toilet—there will be a little fizzing.

To Use: Let baking soda, vinegar, and essential oil sit for 5–15 minutes. Scrub with a toilet brush and flush.

To Store: This is a one-time use product; no storage necessary.

TIME-SAVING TIP

Start with one bathroom and go on to the next. Once you have finished combining the ingredients in your toilets, go back to your first one and scrub. Then move on to each toilet until completed. You can also wipe down the exterior of the toilet bowl with your Lavender and Lemon Bathroom Disinfecting Spray (see recipe earlier in this chapter) or other disinfecting spray while you wait.

Lemon and Peppermint Toilet Cleaning Treatment

16 TABLETS

This is a hands-off cleaning treatment—the best kind! Place a tablet in the toilet bowl, let it fizz and flush it away or let it fizz and give it a little scrub—you decide. Best thing? It smells wonderful. I use them for a quick bathroom cleanup between regular bathroom cleanings. You can pick up the citric acid at the canning section of your grocery store, or look online.

2 CUPS BAKING SODA

⅓ CUP CITRIC ACID

2 TABLESPOONS HYDROGEN PEROXIDE

10 DROPS LEMON ESSENTIAL OIL

10 DROPS PEPPERMINT ESSENTIAL OIL

ICE CUBE TRAY(S)

Variations:

LEMON AND CLOVE — Substitute clove essential oil for the peppermint.

CITRUS — Substitute orange, grapefruit, or lime essential oil for the peppermint.

To Make: Combine ingredients in a bowl and stir—fizzing is normal. Scoop a little less than a tablespoon of the mixture into each ice cube tray compartment. Allow to dry out and harden overnight or in the sun. Once the tablets have hardened, carefully turn the tray over onto a clean surface. The tablets should fall out without any twisting or banging, which could break them into pieces.

To Use: Place 1 tablet in the toilet. Let fizz and sit for 15 minutes and flush or give a little scrub with a toilet brush and flush.

To Store: Store in an airtight glass or plastic container for up to 2 months.

Vinyl Shower Curtain Cleaner

1 CLEAN SHOWER CURTAIN

Vinyl shower curtains can be soap scum and mildew magnets. Did you know that you can wash them in your washing machine?

1 CUP WHITE VINEGAR

To Make: Place white vinegar in your detergent dispenser or directly in the washer for a top-load machine.

To Use: Load 1 or 2 shower curtain liners in and run through a normal cycle using warm water. Line dry or hang right back up in the shower—do not put in the dryer.

To Store: Keep vinegar in your laundry room—there are so many great ways to use this natural product!

TIME-SAVING TIP

Wash a load of rags with the shower curtain liners—you'll have clean rags and a clean shower curtain.

Whirlpool Tub Cleaner

....

1 CLEAN TUB

Getting a whirlpool tub clean can be a challenge. With all the nooks and crannies, it's a little more difficult to clean than standard tubs. Here's an easy method that uses vinegar, dishwasher detergent, and the power of the whirlpool jets to get it clean in a hurry. The dishwasher detergent loosens dirt, soap scum, and mineral deposits, while the white vinegar disinfects.

¼ CUP DISHWASHER POWDER

½ CUP DISTILLED WHITE VINEGAR

To Make: Fill whirlpool tub with hot water, to about 3" above the jets. Add the dishwasher powder, and vinegar to the water.

To Use: Once you've added the detergent and vinegar to the water, turn on the jets to full capacity and run for 15 minutes. Empty and again fill with cold water to 3" above the jets. Run the jets for another 15 minutes to remove any residue. Wipe away any residue with a microfiber cloth. If any gunk remains in the jets or on the handles, use a soft cloth or toothbrush with a little white vinegar to gently wipe away. Rinse and wipe dry.

To Store: This is a one-time-use product; no storage necessary.

HELPFUL HINT

This method of cleaning a whirlpool tub is intended to be completed seasonally. You can wipe your whirlpool tub out weekly or biweekly with the Lavender and Lemon Bathroom Disinfecting Spray (see recipe earlier in this chapter). Then a few times a year use this method to give your whirlpool tub a deep cleaning.

Rust Remover

Rust can hang out in the bathroom around your faucets and fixtures—use this oh-so-simple technique to get rid of it with minimal scrubbing.

DISTILLED WHITE VINEGAR

To Make: Saturate paper towels or cleaning cloths with vinegar.

To Use: Drape wet cloths over rust stains and leave for 15 minutes. Then rub area with the cloth and watch your rust disappear. For tougher stains, use a little Lemon and Clove Scrubbing Sauce (see recipe later in this chapter) after the 15-minute soak.

To Store: This is a one-time-use product; no storage necessary.

TIME-SAVING TIP

Apply the vinegar cloths to your fixtures and faucets while you are taking a shower or cleaning the rest of your bathroom. Give them 15 minutes and you've removed any rusty remnants without scrubbing or using chemicals.

Peppermint and Tea Tree Mold and Mildew Preventer

16 OUNCES

Mold and mildew are common visitors to bathrooms. Forget all those store-bought options—this spray will smell much better and do the same great job!

2 CUPS WATER, DISTILLED OR BOILED AND COOLED

30 DROPS TEA TREE ESSENTIAL OIL

10 DROPS PEPPERMINT ESSENTIAL OIL

To Make: Add ingredients to a spray bottle and shake to combine.

To Use: Spray directly on areas that tend to grow mold or mildew. No rinsing is required. Repeat daily or weekly as needed.

To Store: Store in spray bottle for up to 1 month.

HELPFUL HINT

If mold and mildew are constant problems for you, check to see whether you have proper ventilation. Leave large-scale mold and mildew removal to the experts.

Peppermint and Tea Tree Mold and Mildew Remover

....

16 OUNCES

Have a little mold and mildew in your bathroom? Use this natural solution instead of bleach to get rid of it.

1 CUP WATER, DISTILLED OR BOILED AND COOLED

½ CUP HYDROGEN PEROXIDE

10 DROPS TEA TREE ESSENTIAL OIL

10 DROPS PEPPERMINT ESSENTIAL OIL

Variation:

UNSCENTED — Omit the essential oils.

To Make: Add ingredients to a 16-ounce dark-colored spray bottle and swirl (do not shake) to combine.

To Use: Spray directly on surfaces that have mold or mildew. Let sit for 1–2 hours and rinse.

To Store: Store for up to 1 month in a dark container. (The hydrogen peroxide is light sensitive and will not work as well if exposed to light. You can add a spray top to the hydrogen peroxide container if necessary.)

HELPFUL HINT

Vinegar can also remove mold and mildew. Pour into a spray bottle, and spray on surface and let it sit. No rinsing is necessary.

Vent Cleaner

....

CLEAN VENTS ALL AROUND THE HOUSE

There is something about the vents in bathrooms that attracts a little more dirt and dust that sticks. Here's a simple way to get rid of what a vacuum cleaner attachment leaves behind.

DISTILLED WHITE VINEGAR

Variation:

SCENTED — Add a drop of your favorite essential oil to the vinegar to cut the smell.

To Make: Pour a little vinegar in a small bowl or container.

To Use: Dip your cloth in the white vinegar, wring out any excess, and wipe vents. If you have a vent that's up high, put a sock with a dab of vinegar on a broom handle and carefully wipe.

To Store: Keep white vinegar in your bathroom for cleaning—you'll be glad it's handy!

TIME-SAVING TIP

Use an old (but clean) sock to clean your vents. Fit it right over your hand and dip in the vinegar and clean away! You can also use this technique on other difficult-to-clean areas like window blinds, ceiling fans, and windowsills.

Lemon and Clove Scrubbing Sauce

SCRUBBING POWER FOR 1 BATHROOM

This solution is great for both fixtures and tile.

½ CUP BAKING SODA

¼ CUP DISTILLED WHITE VINEGAR

5 DROPS LEMON ESSENTIAL OIL

5 DROPS CLOVE ESSENTIAL OIL

Variation:

DISINFECTING — Substitute 10 drops tea tree essential oil for the lemon and clove.

To Make: Mix ingredients in a small bowl to make a pastelike consistency. Add more or less vinegar depending on your desired consistency.

To Use: Apply paste to fixtures and any other area that needs a little extra scrubbing.

To Store: This is a one-time-use product; no storage necessary.

Natural Drain Cleaner

....

1 UNCLOGGED DRAIN

Clogged or slow drain causing a mess? Start your teakettle!

¼–½ CUP BAKING SODA

¼–½ CUP DISTILLED WHITE VINEGAR

3 DROPS LEMON ESSENTIAL OIL

1 KETTLEFUL OF BOILING WATER

Variation:

UNSCENTED — Omit the essential oil.

To Make: Put 3 drops essential oil directly down the drain to add a nice scent. Sprinkle baking soda down drain and finish by pouring in distilled white vinegar. Allow to sit for 5–15 minutes.

To Use: Pour hot water down the drain once the solution has done its magic. Then run cold water to see if drain has been cleared. Repeat if necessary.

To Store: This is a one-time-use product; no storage necessary.

TIME-SAVING TIP

Keep your eye on the drain and clean the bathroom at the same time. Once you've cleaned your bathroom, the drain should be unclogged.

CHAPTER 5

RECIPES FOR LAUNDRY

Staring down a pile of laundry is daunting—especially if you've got stains to deal with. Grease, food, grass . . . how can you get everything clean? With organic products, of course! From the recipes in this chapter, choose a soap and softener that fit your laundry lifestyle, and add a stain remover to deal with tough messes. If you use a wrinkle releaser, try a homemade version and you'll be ironing less and enjoying crisp, clean clothes instead. You'll never have to lug giant, heavy bottles of laundry detergent home from the store again!

Lemon and Clove Powdered Laundry Soap—Small Batch

ABOUT 96 LOADS — 1 tablespoon per load for HE machines and 2 tablespoons for regular machines

This soap only takes a few minutes to make, but it yields a whole canister full of great-smelling natural detergent that can last for months. It's natural, it fully dissolves, and it's safe in my high efficiency (HE) washer. I rarely pretreat stains because this formula gets everything out. Grab your piles of laundry and a few simple ingredients and you'll be on a laundry frenzy in no time.

1 5-OUNCE BAR CASTILE SOAP (such as Dr. Bronner's Citrus Orange)

2 CUPS BORAX

2 CUPS ARM & HAMMER SUPER WASHING SODA

1 CUP BAKING SODA

20 DROPS LEMON ESSENTIAL OIL

10 DROPS CLOVE ESSENTIAL OIL

Variations:

UNSCENTED — Use unscented castile soap and don't add any essential oils.

PEPPERMINT AND EUCALYPTUS — Use eucalyptus castile soap, and 20 drops peppermint and 10 drops eucalyptus essential oils.

LAVENDER AND ORANGE — Use lavender castile soap, and 20 drops lavender and 10 drops orange essential oils.

To Make: Grate soap finely (it will yield about 1½ cups of grated soap). Mix all ingredients in a clean garbage bag to minimize mess and to make sure that the detergent is completely combined.

To Use: Put 1 tablespoon of soap for HE machines and 2 tablespoons for regular machines into your washer in the dispenser or machine. Add about 1 tablespoon of Homemade Oxygen Bleach Paste (see recipe later in this chapter) or oxygen bleach powder to any load that needs a little extra stain fighting or whitening.

To Store: Store in an airtight container, about 1-gallon size, for up to 3 months.

TIME-SAVING TIP

Don't have time to grate by hand? Cut the castile soap in 2 or 3 chunks and grate in your food processor instead.

Lemon and Clove Powdered Laundry Soap—Big Batch

ABOUT 288 LOADS—1 tablespoon per load for HE machines and 2 tablespoons for regular machines

3 5-OUNCE BARS CASTILE SOAP (such as Dr. Bronner's Citrus Orange)

6 CUPS BORAX

6 CUPS ARM & HAMMER SUPER WASHING SODA

3 CUPS BAKING SODA

60 DROPS LEMON ESSENTIAL OIL

30 DROPS CLOVE ESSENTIAL OIL

Variations:

UNSCENTED—Use unscented castile soap and don't add any essential oils.

PEPPERMINT AND EUCALYPTUS—Use eucalyptus castile soap, and 60 drops peppermint and 30 drops eucalyptus essential oils.

LAVENDER AND ORANGE—Use lavender castile soap, and 60 drops lavender and 30 drops orange essential oils.

To Make: Grate soap finely (it will yield about 4½ cups of grated soap). Mix all ingredients in a clean garbage bag to minimize mess and to make sure that the detergent is completely combined.

To Use: Put 1 tablespoon of soap for HE machines and 2 tablespoons for regular machines into your washer in the dispenser or machine. Add about 1 tablespoon of Homemade Oxygen Bleach Paste (see recipe later in this chapter) or oxygen bleach powder to any load that needs a little extra stain fighting or whitening.

To Store: Store in a large, airtight container—at least 3 gallons, preferably 5 gallons—for up to 3 months.

Lemon and Lavender Liquid Laundry Soap—Small Batch

ABOUT 20–40 LOADS, DEPENDING ON HOW MUCH SOAP YOU USE

Love the convenience of a liquid laundry detergent but hate the price tag? This recipe will cost you about $1 for an 86-ounce bottle—that's about 3 cents a load!

- ¼ 5-OUNCE BAR CASTILE SOAP (citrus or lavender scented)
- 2 CUPS WATER, PLUS 64 OUNCES HOT WATER
- ¼ CUP BORAX
- ¼ CUP ARM & HAMMER SUPER WASHING SODA
- 10 DROPS LEMON ESSENTIAL OIL
- 10 DROPS LAVENDER ESSENTIAL OIL

Variations:

PEPPERMINT AND EUCALYPTUS — Use eucalyptus castile soap, and 10 drops peppermint and 10 drops eucalyptus essential oils.

LAVENDER AND ORANGE — Use lavender castile soap, and 10 drops lavender and 10 drops orange essential oils.

To Make: Grate soap finely. Place soap, 2 cups water, borax, and soda in a saucepan and heat on low to melt the soap and dissolve the powders. Add essential oils and stir to combine. Pour 64 ounces of hot water into 1 1-gallon or 2 half-gallon containers (this should fill the container(s) about halfway). Fill the rest of the container(s) with melted soap mixture. Close tightly and shake to combine. Let detergent stand overnight before using.

To Use: Add ¼–½ cup of the liquid detergent to a normal load. Every washer is different—reduce the amount if there's too much sudsing, and increase the amount if your clothes need a little more soap.

To Store: Store in original containers or other airtight containers for up to 4 months.

Lemon and Lavender Liquid Laundry Soap—Big Batch

ABOUT 128 LOADS

If you do a lot of laundry, skip the small batch recipe and use this big batch. It's even more cost-effective, and if you have a place to store the jugs, you'll be glad you made extra.

1 5-OUNCE BAR CASTILE SOAP (citrus or lavender scented)

8 CUPS WATER, PLUS 2 GALLONS HOT WATER

1 CUP BORAX

1 CUP ARM & HAMMER SUPER WASHING SODA

40 DROPS LEMON ESSENTIAL OIL

40 DROPS LAVENDER ESSENTIAL OIL

Variations:

PEPPERMINT AND EUCALYPTUS — Use eucalyptus castile soap, and 40 drops peppermint and 40 drops eucalyptus essential oils.

LAVENDER AND ORANGE — Use lavender castile soap, and 40 drops lavender and 40 drops orange essential oils.

To Make: Grate soap finely. Place soap, 8 cups water, borax, and soda in a large stockpot and heat on low to melt the soap and dissolve the powders. Add essential oils and stir to combine. Pour an additional 2 gallons of hot water into 4 1-gallon or 8 half-gallon containers (this should fill the containers about halfway). Fill the rest of the containers with melted soap mixture. Close tightly and shake to combine. Let detergent stand overnight before using.

To Use: Add about ½ cup of the liquid detergent to a normal load. Every washer is different—reduce the amount if there's too much sudsing, and increase the amount if your clothes need a little more soap.

To Store: Store in original containers or other airtight containers for up to 4 months.

Lemon and Clove Fabric Softener—Liquid

If fabric softener is a necessity on your laundry day, you'll love this formula. Not only will your laundry be softened, but it will smell good, too.

1 GALLON DISTILLED WHITE VINEGAR

2 CUPS BAKING SODA

20 DROPS LEMON ESSENTIAL OIL

20 DROPS CLOVE ESSENTIAL OIL

Variations:

UNSCENTED — Omit the essential oils.

CONDITIONER — If you want to make your homemade fabric softener look a little more like store-bought, add 2–3 cups of hair conditioner to this formula. This will change the amount of softener produced, but per load measurements are the same.

LEMON AND LAVENDER — Substitute 20 drops lavender essential oil for the clove.

To Make: Pour vinegar in a large bowl or container for mixing. Add baking soda and essential oils and stir to combine. Pour back in vinegar container for storage, or use a different container if desired.

To Use: Add ¼–½ cup per load.

To Store: Store in airtight container for up to 3 months.

HELPFUL HINT

Prefer a dryer sheet instead of a liquid? Spray this softener on a small cotton cloth and toss it in with your laundry, or saturate a sheet with the softener and let it dry thoroughly. Add the sheet to your laundry until the smell and effects dissipate, then use a new one.

Fabric Softener—Vinegar

ABOUT 64 LOADS

Did you know that you can use vinegar in the rinse cycle to soften fabrics? Add some essential oil and you've got a great (and cheap) fabric softener.

16-OUNCE BOTTLE OF WHITE VINEGAR

50 DROPS ESSENTIAL OILS OF YOUR CHOICE

Variations:

UNSCENTED — Omit essential oils.

LEMON AND CLOVE — Use 30 drops lemon and 20 drops clove essential oils.

To Make: Add essential oils to white vinegar bottle. Cover and shake to combine.

To Use: Add ¼ cup of the softener per load. Depending on your machine, add in the softener dispenser, in the rinse cycle, or in a softener ball.

To Store: Store indefinitely.

Wrinkle Releaser

If you're an avid wrinkle-releaser user, you'll love this natural recipe. No chemicals, just a little wrinkle-releasing action. The vodka helps to speed the drying process of the wrinkle releaser. Spray on your clothes, give them a little tug, and be amazed!

1 CUP WATER, DISTILLED OR BOILED AND COOLED

1 TEASPOON FABRIC SOFTENER, SUCH AS LEMON AND CLOVE FABRIC SOFTENER (see recipe earlier in this chapter)

1 TEASPOON VODKA

To Make: Add ingredients to a spray bottle and shake to combine.

To Use: Hang clothing to be wrinkle-released on a hanger. (Always test delicate fabric first.) Using a very light mist, evenly spray with wrinkle releaser from top to bottom. Tug and smooth and allow to air-dry.

To Store: Store in spray bottle for up to 3 months.

Design-a-Scent Dryer Sheet

1 REUSABLE SHEET

Love the lingering scents of dryer sheets? Try this easy and natural solution. Create your own signature scent, or try one of the suggested combinations.

6" × 6" COTTON OR WOOL SQUARE
(recycled T-shirts, sweaters, or socks will work)

2–4 DROPS ESSENTIAL OILS

Variations:

LEMON AND CLOVE — Use 2 drops lemon and 2 drops clove essential oils.

LEMON AND LAVENDER — Use 2 drops lemon and 2 drops lavender essential oils.

To Make: Place cotton square in a glass or plastic container. Dispense essential oils on fabric square. Allow essential oils to dry thoroughly.

To Use: Place dryer sheet on top of wet clothes in dryer and dry as usual.

To Store: Store in jar or container in laundry room in between dryer uses. When sheet has lost its scent, add more oil as above.

HELPFUL HINT

Don't use more than 4 drops of essential oil on the dryer sheet and don't store your essential oil bottles near your dryer—oil is flammable.

HE Washing Machine Cleaner

1 CLEAN HE WASHING MACHINE

Despite all the benefits of high efficiency (HE) machines, HE washing machine owners have one common complaint: bad-smelling laundry. One simple cleaning task will eliminate the problem and keep your washer in great condition as well. HE washers use less water and less energy, but they can create mildew, mold, and detergent residue buildup. Some washers have a separate cleaning cycle as an option, so use that if yours falls into that category. If not, all you need is some chlorine-free bleach, vinegar, and a little time.

¾ CUP CHLORINE-FREE BLEACH

VINEGAR

To Make: Choose the hottest water setting on your machine and the extra rinse option if your machine has that. Add chlorine-free bleach to the bleach dispenser.

To Use: Run wash cycle and then repeat without the chlorine-free bleach. Clean the dispensers with a cloth dampened with white vinegar. Dry thoroughly before reinserting. Don't forget the rubber seal—wipe it down with a cloth dampened in white vinegar and dry thoroughly. Finish by wiping down the entire exterior of your washing machine.

To Store: This is a one-time-use product; no storage necessary.

HELPFUL HINT

Repeat this process monthly and you'll eliminate the stinky laundry and keep your HE washing machine in tip-top shape. Always keep the washing machine door open when it's not in use to keep the mildew away.

Regular Washing Machine Cleaner

1 CLEAN AND MILDEW-FREE WASHING MACHINE

Cleaning a washing machine may seem like an oxymoron, but make it part of your cleaning routine. Making sure that the machine is clean will ensure that your clothes and towels don't have any lingering odors and that you have removed any extra detergent that's stuck in nooks and crannies.

4 CUPS DISTILLED WHITE VINEGAR

To Make: Fill washing machine with the hottest water, choose the longest cycle and largest load setting, and add the vinegar. Open the lid or pause the cycle to allow the vinegar to sit and work its magic for at least an hour.

To Use: While the vinegar is working, dip a cleaning cloth in the vinegar solution and wipe down the exterior of the washing machine. Remove any compartments that you are able to and clean those as well. Once an hour has passed, let the washing machine complete the cycle. Wipe any remaining missed areas once the machine has run its cycle. Leave the door/lid open to let the interior dry thoroughly. If any odors remain, run another cycle without the vinegar.

To Store: This is a one-time-use product; no storage necessary.

Pretreat Goo

4 OUNCES

If you like your pretreater to be in a liquid-y gel form, you'll love this recipe. Mix it up right along with your liquid laundry detergent to save time. I like to use it on food stains on my kids' clothing. It stays where it's applied and gets all those mystery stains right out.

1 TABLESPOON BORAX

½ CUP LIQUID LAUNDRY DETERGENT
(such as Lemon and Lavender Liquid Laundry Soap—see recipe earlier in this chapter)

To Make: Mix detergent and borax and pour into small squirt bottle—a recycled glue bottle works great! Shake to make sure that the borax is dissolved.

To Use: Squirt directly on stain, rub into stain, and let sit for at least 15 minutes. Launder as usual.

To Store: Store in squirt bottle for up to 1 month.

Pillow Cleaner

3–4 CLEAN PILLOWS

Did you know that you can wash your pillows? Most synthetic and down pillows are safe to launder, but just to be safe, double-check the tags on yours before giving it a try. Washing your pillows a few times a year will ensure you always have clean, fresh pillows on your beds.

DETERGENT, SUCH AS LEMON AND CLOVE POWDERED LAUNDRY SOAP (see recipe earlier in this chapter)

1–2 TABLESPOONS HOMEMADE OXYGEN BLEACH PASTE (see recipe later in this chapter)

To Make: Place pillows in your washing machine. Take care not to overfill your machine—most machines can handle 2 pillows, but if you have a large-capacity washer you can probably fit 3 or 4.

To Use: Add detergent and whitener to your washing machine. Choose the hottest setting and wash as a normal load. Before removing pillows, check to see if they are holding extra water. If they are, you may need to run a second spin cycle. Dry in your dryer on high, rotating once or twice to ensure that they dry thoroughly and evenly.

To Store: This is a one-time-use product; no storage necessary.

HELPFUL HINT

Put a pillow protector on your pillows—this will keep the skin oils and sweat off your pillows and the dust mites away, in turn keeping the pillows cleaner for longer.

Lemon Natural Whitener

This is a great bleach alternative for cloth diapers, antique linens, and other washable delicates. Try this on a warm and sunny day when you can dry the clothes outside on a clothesline, and you'll reap the benefits of lemons and sun combined.

THE JUICE OF 1 LEMON, ABOUT ¼–½ CUP

1 GALLON HOT WATER

To Make: Squeeze the juice of a lemon in a gallon of hot water.

To Use: Combine 1 gallon hot water and the juice of one lemon in a bucket, laundry tub, or washing machine. Let your clothes soak for 1–2 hours. Run through the rinse cycle and set out in the sun to dry. The sun will work with the lemon to naturally whiten the whites. Wash afterwards as usual.

To Store: This is a one-time-use product; no storage necessary.

Whitening Gel

3 TABLESPOONS

This recipe is most effective on white clothing with organic stains like juice, berries, and wine, but you can try it on any white clothing with any kind of stain and watch the stain disappear before your eyes.

2 TABLESPOONS HYDROGEN PEROXIDE

1 TABLESPOON ARM & HAMMER SUPER WASHING SODA

To Make: Mix hydrogen peroxide and Super Washing Soda in a small bowl. Microwave on high for 10–20 seconds to dissolve the washing soda. The solution will fizz up, so keep an eye on it. Stir to combine and help dissolve.

To Use: Apply directly to stain. Let sit for at least 15 minutes and launder as usual.

To Store: This is a one-time-use product; no storage necessary (hydrogen peroxide will lose its effectiveness within a few hours).

TIME-SAVING TIP

Keep track of which clothes have stains by putting a stain basket in your laundry room. Pretreat and soak, or save them up and treat them all at once.

No-Bleach Laundry Whitener and Brightener

1 LOAD

If you're reaching for the bleach, instead turn to this one natural ingredient—hydrogen peroxide! It's known for its bleaching properties and it's safe to use in the laundry room.

2 OUNCES OR ¼ CUP HYDROGEN PEROXIDE

To Make: Add this to the bleach compartment on your HE washing machine, or directly to the water if you have a regular machine.

To Use: Launder as usual. Treat hydrogen peroxide like bleach—do not use it anywhere near your brights or colors.

To Store: Keep a bottle of hydrogen peroxide in your laundry room if you have lots of whites to whiten.

Stain Spray—General

Here's a great two-ingredient spray for fresh or set-in stains—keep a small bottle in your laundry room for pretreating.

8 OUNCES WATER, DISTILLED OR BOILED AND SLIGHTLY COOLED

2 TABLESPOONS BORAX

To Make: Add borax to a spray bottle and pour warm water over borax. Shake thoroughly to combine.

To Use: Spray directly on stain. Launder as usual.

To Store: Store for up to 1 month.

MONEY-SAVING TIP

Keep a piece of white chalkboard chalk in your laundry room to pretreat any little grease stains—the chalk absorbs the grease.

Tea Tree Stain Stick

1 STICK, ABOUT 3 OUNCES

If you prefer your stain removal in stick form, use this recipe. Tea tree is a mild solvent and will help to dissolve set-in stains.

½ 5-OUNCE BAR CASTILE SOAP

3 TEASPOONS WATER

4 DROPS TEA TREE ESSENTIAL OIL

To Make: Grate soap; place in microwave-safe bowl and add 3 teaspoons of water. Melt on low heat in microwave in 30-second intervals for about a minute and a half. Stir and check every 30 seconds. (Depending on your microwave, this may take longer, but it will melt.) Once it has melted, let cool for 5 minutes and stir in essential oil. Pour in a clean container with a push-up bottom—like an old cleaned-out stain stick container or deodorant container. Allow to cool to a solid state before using.

To Use: Spread a little stain stick on any stains and launder as usual.

To Store: Store in a cool place to avoid softening for up to 6 months.

Homemade Oxygen Bleach Paste

1 LOAD OF LAUNDRY

This inexpensive alternative to the store-bought version works just as well!

1 TABLESPOON HYDROGEN PEROXIDE

1 TABLESPOON WASHING SODA

To Make: Mix peroxide and washing soda together in a small bowl. The consistency should be a dry paste, and not powdery.

To Use: Add a little water to the bowl before putting the bleach in the detergent dispenser or directly into the washing machine water.

To Store: After the ingredients are mixed they lose their effectiveness in a few hours, so use it right away. Store peroxide and soda separately in your laundry room.

TIME-SAVING TIP

Doing multiple loads on laundry day? Mix ½ cup of peroxide and ½ cup of washing soda in a small container and add 2 tablespoons per load.

Pet Stain Remover

4 OUNCES

We all love our pets, but sometimes those pet stains can be tough to remove. This recipe works on dog beds, blankets, and other launderable pet products. The vinegar cleans and sanitizes while the baking soda neutralizes odors.

½ CUP DISTILLED WHITE VINEGAR

½ CUP BAKING SODA

¼ CUP LAUNDRY DETERGENT (either liquid or powder)

To Make: Mix ingredients together in a bowl or container (fizzing is normal).

To Use: Pretreat any obvious stains. Pour solution directly in detergent dispenser (for HE machines) or in your washing machine (for regular machines). Launder on hot, and use the soak option on your machine if you have it. Dry as usual.

To Store: This is a one-time-use product; no storage necessary.

HELPFUL HINT

Once you have laundered your pet stains away, clean your washing machine to get rid of any pet hair, dander, and other pet-related germs. Use the HE Washing Machine Cleaner or Regular Washing Machine Cleaner recipe given earlier in this chapter.

CHAPTER 6

RECIPES FOR BEDROOMS AND LIVING SPACES

Keeping the most-used spaces in your home neat and tidy creates a welcoming environment and allows you to truly relax. If you're always looking at piles and messes while you're trying to relax after a day of work, decluttering will help, but so will some great natural and organic cleaning recipes. Fresh scents, true cleanliness, and safe and easy-to-make formulas will have you happy to be cleaning again. If you love air fresheners, you can create your own versions with essential oils. Really! In this chapter, you'll find ways to clean up life's little and big messes with ease.

Lavender Mattress Freshener

1 FRESH MATTRESS AND A GOOD NIGHT'S SLEEP

Need to freshen your mattress and want to get a good night's sleep to boot? Freshen your mattress with this super-easy recipe.

1 CUP BAKING SODA

3–4 DROPS LAVENDER ESSENTIAL OIL

Variation:

UNSCENTED — Omit the essential oil.

To Make: Combine the baking soda and essential oil.

To Use: Sprinkle on mattress. Allow to sit and absorb any odors for at least 30 minutes. Use the hose attachment on your vacuum cleaner to vacuum up the powder.

To Store: You can store any extra indefinitely or place in your bedroom closet to absorb any odors until the next time you need to freshen your mattress.

TIME-SAVING TIP

Use a cleaned-out sprinkle-top container to evenly distribute the freshener.

Peppermint and Lavender Linen Refresher

12 OUNCES

This linen refresher is perfect for hiding smells on pillows, bedding, and clothing—and it is also a little aromatherapy in a bottle! Spray on your pillow before bed for a restful night's sleep.

1 CUP WATER
½ CUP VODKA
10 DROPS LAVENDER ESSENTIAL OIL
5 DROPS PEPPERMINT ESSENTIAL OIL

Variation:

LAVENDER AND LEMON — Substitute lemon essential oil for the peppermint.

To Make: Combine ingredients and pour into a 16-ounce container with a spray top.

To Use: Spray about 8" away from any linen that needs a little freshening.

To Store: Store in spray bottle in a cool place for up to 2 months.

Citrus Wood Cleaner and Polish

This is practically an aromatherapy session in a cleaner. The essential oils are the powerhouse in this concoction, and they help to clean and polish any wood furniture back to a beautiful shine. You'll love how fresh and citrusy this cleaner and polish is!

⅓ CUP OLIVE, ALMOND, OR
   FRACTIONATED COCONUT OIL

½ CUP WATER, DISTILLED OR BOILED
   AND COOLED

10 DROPS ORANGE ESSENTIAL OIL

30 DROPS LEMON ESSENTIAL OIL

To Make: Add water and oil to a lidded container or spray bottle. Shake to combine and add essential oils. Shake thoroughly before using, as this is oil and water and will naturally separate.

To Use: Shake thoroughly. Pour or spray a little bit of this cleaner on a microfiber cloth and start dusting. When your cloth gets dusty, give it a shake outside and add a little more cleaner to your cloth. Continue cleaning and polishing.

To Store: Store in a cool, dark place for up to 2 weeks.

Lemon Wood Polish

I use this concoction seasonally when I want to oil my furniture from top to bottom to condition it and keep it looking great. I find that this is just a little more than I need to oil all the furniture in my house. The lemon peels provide natural essential oil.

LEMON PEELS FROM 1 LEMON

¼ CUP LEMON JUICE

½ CUP ALMOND, OLIVE, OR FRACTIONATED COCONUT OIL

To Make: Use a vegetable peeler to peel thin strips of a lemon rind. Mix lemon juice, oil, and peels in an airtight, lidded container. Shake to combine. Let rest overnight to release the essential oil of the fresh lemon peels.

To Use: Pour a small amount of the polish on a clean dusting cloth and polish. I love using microfiber for dusting and polishing because it collects and keeps lint and dust in its fibers.

To Store: Use immediately or store for up to 1 week in the refrigerator. Let mixture come up to room temperature before using.

Citrus Wood Cleaner

Have some furniture that needs a little cleaning? Score big at the flea market? This formula is great for cleaning dirty and dusty furniture and the almond oil will give your furniture a little shine, too.

¼ CUP WHITE VINEGAR

2 TABLESPOONS ALMOND OIL

5 DROPS LEMON ESSENTIAL OIL

5 DROPS CITRUS ESSENTIAL OIL

To Make: Mix ingredients in a small bowl or jar.

To Use: Dip a microfiber cleaning cloth in the solution and wipe furniture. Buff in a circular motion to remove any residual oil.

To Store: This is a one-time-use product; no storage necessary.

Citrus Microfiber Wood Cleaning Cloths

4 CLOTHS

If you're looking to infuse a little all-natural essential oil into your wood cleaning, this is a great solution. The citrus scent leaves your room smelling fresh and clean, and the concentration of lemon rind and essential oil eliminates the vinegar smell.

4 MICROFIBER CLOTHS

1 CUP WATER, DISTILLED OR BOILED AND COOLED

½ CUP WHITE VINEGAR

2 TEASPOONS ALMOND OIL

RIND OF 1 LEMON

RIND OF 1 ORANGE

10 DROPS LEMON ESSENTIAL OIL

To Make: Combine liquids in a jar, then place clean microfiber cloths and lemon and orange rinds in the container. Swirl liquid around in the container and pour off excess, squeezing cloths to get excess liquid out of container. Cloths should be barely damp.

To Use: Wring out excess liquid (there shouldn't be much) and wipe down wood furniture as needed.

To Store: Keep cloths in sealed, airtight container for 1–2 weeks.

TIME-SAVING TIP

Use a vegetable peeler to quickly remove the rind off your citrus fruits (lemon and orange work great!) and leave the white pith behind.

Disposable Citrus Furniture Wipes—Wood

24 WIPES

Want the convenience of a wipe for your wood furniture? Here's a great recipe.

12 THICK AND DURABLE PAPER TOWELS (such as Bounty DuraTowels)

¼ CUP WHITE VINEGAR

1 TABLESPOON ALMOND OIL

5 DROPS LEMON ESSENTIAL OIL

5 DROPS CITRUS ESSENTIAL OIL

1 CUP WATER (boiled and cooled, or distilled if storing for longer than a couple of days)

Variation:

UNSCENTED—Omit the essential oils.

To Make: Tear off about a dozen paper towels, cut them in half, and stack into a neat pile. Roll up the paper towels and stuff them in a 2-cup, wide-mouth mason jar. Mix the ingredients in a large measuring cup and pour over the paper towels in the mason jar. Put the lid on and shake and swirl the liquid around to make sure that it is absorbed into the paper towels. (A large zip-top bag or baby wipe container also works for storing these wipes if you don't have a mason jar—the bag will save space as well.)

To Use: Carefully remove a wipe or two, wipe furniture, and buff any oil with a microfiber cleaning cloth.

To Store: Store in a sealed, airtight container for up to 1 week.

Natural Scratch Remover

Have a few minutes? Mix up this simple scratch remover and buff away those scratches on your wood furniture. The lemon juice and vinegar combine to help remove shallow scratches or minimize the look of deeper scratches.

1 TEASPOON LEMON JUICE

1 TEASPOON DISTILLED WHITE VINEGAR

To Make: Mix lemon juice and vinegar together in a small bowl.

To Use: Dip cloth in solution and rub into scratches until they disappear. Buff away any residue with a dry cloth.

To Store: This is a one-time-use product; no storage necessary.

Leather Wipes

If you prefer the convenience of a wipe for cleaning, try this solution on your leather furniture. Always test your cleaners on an inconspicuous area first to make sure there isn't any discoloring.

12 THICK AND DURABLE PAPER TOWELS (such as Bounty DuraTowels)

3 TABLESPOONS ALMOND OIL

½ CUP VINEGAR

½ CUP WATER, DISTILLED OR BOILED AND COOLED

To Make: Tear off about a dozen paper towels, cut them in half, and stack into a neat pile. Roll up the paper towels and stuff them in a 2-cup, wide-mouth mason jar. Mix the ingredients in a large measuring cup and pour over the paper towels in the mason jar. Put the lid on and shake and swirl the liquid around to make sure that it is absorbed into the paper towels. Pour off excess, as this wipe works better a little on the dry side. (A large zip-top bag or baby wipe container also works for storing these wipes if you don't have a mason jar—the bag will save space as well.)

To Use: Carefully remove a wipe or two, wring out any excess cleaner in your sink, and use as you would any cleaning wipe.

To Store: Store in a sealed, airtight container for up to 1 week.

Peppermint Glass and Mirror Wipes

Sometimes you don't want to bother with a spray bottle—in that case, use these wipes!

12 THICK AND DURABLE PAPER TOWELS (such as Bounty DuraTowels)

1 CUP WATER, DISTILLED OR BOILED AND COOLED

1 TABLESPOON DISTILLED WHITE VINEGAR

2 TABLESPOONS RUBBING ALCOHOL

5 DROPS PEPPERMINT ESSENTIAL OIL

Variation:

UNSCENTED—Omit the essential oil.

To Make: Tear off about a dozen paper towels, cut them in half, and stack into a neat pile. Roll up the paper towels and stuff them in a 2-cup, wide-mouth mason jar. Mix the ingredients in a large measuring cup and pour over the paper towels in the mason jar. Put the lid on and shake and swirl the liquid around to make sure that it is absorbed into the paper towels. Pour off excess, as this wipe works better a little on the dry side. (A large zip-top bag or baby wipe container also works for storing these wipes if you don't have a mason jar—the bag will save space as well.)

To Use: Carefully remove a wipe or two, wring out any excess cleaner in your sink, and use as you would any cleaning wipe.

To Store: Store in a sealed, airtight container for up to 1 week.

Lemon and Peppermint
All-Purpose Cleaning Wipes

24 WIPES

Wipe obsessed? You'll love this great all-purpose cleaning wipe. It has a fresh citrusy scent that's sure to brighten any cleaning task.

12 THICK AND DURABLE PAPER TOWELS (such as Bounty DuraTowels)

¼ CUP WHITE VINEGAR

5 DROPS LEMON ESSENTIAL OIL

5 DROPS PEPPERMINT ESSENTIAL OIL

2 CUPS WATER (boiled and cooled, or distilled if storing for longer than a couple of days)

Variation:

UNSCENTED — Omit the essential oils.

To Make: Tear off about a dozen paper towels, cut them in half, and stack into a neat pile. Roll up the paper towels and stuff them in a 2-cup, wide-mouth mason jar. Mix the ingredients in a large measuring cup and pour over the paper towels in the mason jar. Put the lid on and shake and swirl the liquid around to make sure that it is absorbed into the paper towels. (A large zip-top bag or baby wipe container also works for storing these wipes if you don't have a mason jar—the bag will save space as well.)

To Use: Carefully remove a wipe or two, wring out any excess cleaner in your sink, and use as you would any cleaning wipe.

To Store: Store in a sealed, airtight container for up to 1 week.

Peppermint and Tea Tree Antibacterial Wipes

24 WIPES

Want the reassurance of knowing that you've disinfected with a cleaning wipe? Here's a great recipe you'll make again and again. The vinegar and vodka have natural germ-killing properties.

12 THICK AND DURABLE PAPER TOWELS (such as Bounty DuraTowels)

¼ CUP WHITE VINEGAR

¼ CUP VODKA

5 DROPS PEPPERMINT ESSENTIAL OIL

5 DROPS TEA TREE ESSENTIAL OIL

1 CUP BOILED AND SLIGHTLY COOLED WATER

Variation:

UNSCENTED — Omit the essential oils.

To Make: Tear off about a dozen paper towels, cut them in half, and stack into a neat pile. Roll up the paper towels and stuff them in a 2-cup, wide-mouth mason jar. Mix the ingredients in a large measuring cup and pour over the paper towels in the mason jar. Put the lid on and shake and swirl the liquid around to make sure that it is absorbed into the paper towels. (A large zip-top bag or baby wipe container also works for storing these wipes if you don't have a mason jar—the bag will save space as well.)

To Use: Carefully remove a wipe or two, and use as you would any cleaning wipe. Wipe surface thoroughly and allow it to remain wet for 5–10 minutes—this is necessary for the antibacterial properties to kick in. Use freely on hard surfaces where germ killing is necessary—remotes, light switches, and counters are great places to start.

To Store: Store in a sealed, airtight container for up to 1 week.

Lavender and Lemon Pet Foot Wipes

12 WIPES

Pets in the house can wreak havoc on your cleaning regime—keep these wipes near the door to wipe off muddy paws right when Spot walks in. The lavender and lemon essential oils are calming, odor-reducing, and safe for pets. Keep essential oil bottles out of the "reach" of your furry friends, though.

12 SMALL, COTTON WASHCLOTHS

1½ CUPS WATER, DISTILLED OR BOILED AND COOLED

2 TEASPOONS–1 TABLESPOON CASTILE SOAP

2 DROPS LAVENDER ESSENTIAL OIL

2 DROPS LEMON ESSENTIAL OIL

Variation:
UNSCENTED — Omit the essential oils.

To Make: Place washcloths in a large glass or plastic container with a lid. Mix the ingredients in a large measuring cup and pour over the cloths in the container. Put the lid on and shake and swirl the liquid around to make sure that it is absorbed into the cloths. Pour out excess. A large zip-top bag, mason jar, or baby wipe container also works for storing these foot wipes.

To Use: Remove cloth and squeeze out any excess liquid. Wipe paws and launder washcloth.

To Store: Store in a sealed, airtight container for up to 1 week.

Lemon and Clove Air Freshener Spray

12 OUNCES

Keep this spray handy for any time a room needs a little freshening up. You'll love the lemon and clove combination—it's the perfect blend of fresh and cozy.

1 CUP WATER, DISTILLED OR BOILED AND COOLED

½ CUP VODKA

5–10 DROPS LEMON ESSENTIAL OIL— start with 5 drops and give it a spray. Add more essential oil to your liking if needed.

5–10 DROPS CLOVE ESSENTIAL OIL— start with 5 drops and give it a spray. Add more essential oil to your liking if needed.

To Make: Add ingredients to a spray bottle and shake to combine.

To Use: Spray 2 or 3 sprays in any room that needs a little freshening.

To Store: Store in spray bottle in a cool place for up to 2 months.

Cinnamon and Spice Air Freshener Simmer

1 SIMMER

Love the smell of baking but don't want to bake? Try this spicy simmer! It's perfect if you're having company over, or if you're having an open house to try to sell your home.

4 CUPS WATER

PEEL FROM 1 LEMON

3 CINNAMON STICKS

1 WHOLE NUTMEG

10–12 WHOLE CLOVES OR 5 DROPS CLOVE ESSENTIAL OIL

DASH OF VANILLA EXTRACT

Variation:

ROSEMARY AND LEMON — Prefer a savory smell? Add rosemary leaves instead of the spices.

To Make: Combine ingredients in a large saucepan.

To Use: Let simmer on low for 1–2 hours. Make sure you keep an eye on the pan. Discard when simmer has completed.

To Store: This is a one-time-use product; no storage necessary.

TIME-SAVING TIP

If you know you'll use this recipe multiple times in the next month or so, you can combine the spices in a jar and store that portion of the recipe. When you're ready to simmer, just combine water, lemon peel, and vanilla extract with a portion of spices and proceed with your simmer.

Microfiber Furniture Cleaning Kit

1 CLEAN SOFA OR CHAIR

Microfiber is appealing because of its durability and how it seems to be impervious to wear and tear. But if you own microfiber upholstery, you know that it does attract dirt and fingerprints. Cleaning microfiber requires 3 ingredients and just a few steps.

4–8 OUNCES RUBBING ALCOHOL

WHITE OR LIGHT-COLORED SPONGE WITH A SCRUBBING SURFACE

BRISTLED CLEANING BRUSH WITH WHITE BRISTLES

To Make: Pour rubbing alcohol in a spray bottle.

To Use: Remove cushions from the furniture. Using a hose attachment, vacuum all crumbs and dirt from the sofa or chair. Make sure you vacuum the arms, front, and back of the sofa or chair as well. Then clean one small section at a time. Spray the alcohol on the surface and, using the textured side of the sponge, scrub the surface. Repeat this process until the entire piece of furniture is clean. Let the entire piece of furniture dry thoroughly. The last step is to fluff up the fibers by lightly scrubbing with the scrubbing brush. Use a circular motion so you don't see any brush strokes. Continue doing this until your furniture is uniformly brushed and your furniture will look good as new!

To Store: This is a one-time-use product; no storage necessary.

Lemon and Clove Furniture Freshening Spray

If your furniture has a little odor, give it a little spray of this—the vodka will kill germs and the essential oils will eliminate the scent.

½ CUP WATER, DISTILLED OR BOILED AND COOLED

½ CUP VODKA

5 DROPS LEMON ESSENTIAL OIL—
start with 5 drops and give it a spray. Add more essential oil to your liking if needed.

5 DROPS CLOVE ESSENTIAL OIL—
start with 5 drops and give it a spray. Add more essential oil to your liking if needed.

To Make: Add ingredients to a spray bottle and shake to combine.

To Use: Spray 2 or 3 sprays on any furniture that needs a little odor removal. Always spot-test your furniture in an inconspicuous place to make sure that the spray doesn't leave a residue or cause discoloration.

To Store: Store in a cool place for up to 2 months.

Leather Cleaner

Leather may not always show its dirty side, but rest assured, the dirt is in there! Once you see how much dirt you can lift off, you'll be inclined to clean it more often.

1 TEASPOON CASTILE SOAP

1 CUP WATER, DISTILLED OR BOILED AND COOLED

To Make: Combine ingredients and place in a bottle with a cap.

To Use: Shake thoroughly and pour onto a cotton cleaning cloth. Wipe clean in small sections and dry immediately.

To Store: Store for up to 1 month.

Leather Scratch Remover

A FEW DROPS

I love the look of leather furniture, but I'm not fond of the very visible scratches that sometimes appear. Whether they're from a pet's claws or a toy truck, those scratches will be gone in a snap with this super-simple remedy.

OLIVE OR ALMOND OIL

To Make: Pour 1 or 2 drops of the oil on your cloth.

To Use: Rub oil into leather until scratch disappears. Wipe off any excess with a dry cloth.

To Store: Store oils in a cool, dark place.

Upholstered Fabric Cleaner

This recipe is for those times when you just washed the pillows on your sofa and some-one spills a little drop of chocolate milk on one. It doesn't need to be fully laundered, but you don't want the stain sitting there.

2 TEASPOONS CASTILE SOAP

¼ CUP WARM WATER

To Make: Mix warm water and castile soap in a small cup or container.

To Use: Dip cotton cloth (preferably white) in the water and castile soap mixture. Dab away the stain. Once the stain is removed, dab with a clean, dry cloth to absorb any liquid. Add a little water to wipe away any residual soap.

To Store: This is a one-time-use product; no storage necessary.

Electronics Wipes

6 WIPES

If you want to make your own electronics cleaning wipes, try this recipe. It'll make cleaning your screens, computer mouse, and keypads a breeze. Using distilled water ensures that no mineral deposits end up on your screens.

6 SMALL CLEANING CLOTHS—
microfiber works great

¼ CUP RUBBING ALCOHOL

½ CUP DISTILLED WATER

To Make: Mix solution in container. Add wipes and pour out solution. Squeeze cloths to get rid of most of the excess solution.

To Use: Take out a cloth, and squeeze out any excess solution. (Cloth should be barely damp.) Wipe screens, from top to bottom and left to right.

To Store: Store in airtight container for 1 month.

TIME-SAVING TIP

When one screen is dirty, you might as well take the time to wipe all screens while you've got a wipe out—this formula works on computer screens, television screens, mice, keyboards, remotes, and other electronic devices.

Electronics Cleaning Solution

8 OUNCES

With this easy (and cheap!) solution, you'll have clean screens throughout your home and office and never have to buy a pre-made electronics cleaner again. The distilled water ensures that no mineral deposits end up on your screens.

½ CUP RUBBING ALCOHOL

½ CUP DISTILLED WATER

To Make: Add ingredients to a spray bottle and shake to combine.

To Use: Spray directly on microfiber cloth—do not spray on screens. Wipe from top to bottom and left to right.

To Store: Store in spray bottle for 2 months or longer.

Essential Oil Air Freshener

4 OUNCES, FOR USE IN 1 OR 2 CONTAINERS

Artificial fragrances and perfumes can be harmful to breathe and can increase sensitivities in people with allergies and asthma. If you like an air freshener and want a safe alternative, you'll love this recipe.

¼ CUP ALMOND OIL

¼ CUP VODKA

10 DROPS ORANGE ESSENTIAL OIL

5 DROPS LEMON ESSENTIAL OIL

5 DROPS CLOVE ESSENTIAL OIL

REEDS—look for 12" reed diffuser replacement sticks on Amazon.com

SMALL GLASS CONTAINER WITH A NARROW NECK—like a short vase or small decanter

Variations:

LEMON AND CLOVE — Use 10 drops lemon and 10 drops clove essential oils.

LAVENDER AND MINT — Use 10 drops lavender and 10 drops peppermint essential oils.

To Make: Mix oil and vodka together to combine. Add essential oils—you can reduce the amount or change the scents based on your taste.

To Use: Pour air freshener in glass container, add reeds, and set aside to freshen air. Keep out of reach of children and pets.

To Store: Keep on counter or shelf until scent no longer remains—up to 2 months.

HELPFUL HINT

Place a drop of essential oil on a light bulb and turn the light bulb on. The warmth from the bulb will activate a secret, subtle scent.

CHAPTER 7

RECIPES FOR FLOORS

When you've got unexpected company coming over—what do you clean first? I run for the bathrooms and check the floors. Clean floors will make your whole house feel cleaner, but it can be difficult to figure out the best cleaning solution for different floor types. Whether you have vinyl, carpet, or hardwood, you can clean it safely, effectively, and organically. And you can rest easy knowing that you're also saving money. How's that for a clean sweep?

Citrus Carpet Freshener

2 CUPS

This is one of my favorite homemade cleaning solutions. It keeps my carpets smelling fresh no matter how busy my house gets!

2 CUPS BAKING SODA

10 DROPS LEMON ESSENTIAL OIL

10 DROPS ORANGE OR GRAPEFRUIT ESSENTIAL OIL

Variations:

UNSCENTED — Omit essential oils.

LEMON AND CLOVE — Substitute 10 drops clove for the orange or grapefruit essential oil.

To Make: Add baking soda to a glass jar or container and scent with essential oils. Stir to combine.

To Use: Sprinkle on carpet or rug. Let sit for 15 minutes and vacuum thoroughly.

To Store: Keep in a cool, dark place indefinitely.

MONEY-SAVING TIP

This homemade carpet freshener costs pennies to make (much cheaper than commercial versions!), mixes up in a minute, and keeps indefinitely.

Odor Absorber

If you have an odor in your carpet and you can't get rid of it, you don't want to mask it with another scent. Just grab that box of baking soda—it's the ultimate natural odor absorber.

BAKING SODA

To Make: No mixing required, just sprinkle!

To Use: Simply sprinkle baking soda on the carpet or rug and let it sit for at least 24 hours. Cover the spot so a pet or small child doesn't disturb the baking soda. Vacuum up residue and repeat if necessary.

To Store: Keep baking soda on hand for all of your odor-absorbing needs. Keeps indefinitely.

MONEY-SAVING TIP

Baking soda's baking qualities have a shelf life, but you can still use the baking soda for cleaning and neutralizing odors. Instead of tossing an "expired" box of baking soda, repurpose it for your carpet care.

Peppermint Laminate Floor Cleaner

Streaks abound when you use commercial floor cleaners. This concoction will not only clean your floors, it will leave them streak-free and smelling great.

5 OUNCES WATER

5 OUNCES DISTILLED WHITE VINEGAR

5 OUNCES RUBBING ALCOHOL

10 DROPS PEPPERMINT ESSENTIAL OIL

To Make: Mix liquid and pour in a container with a spray top, or pour mixture in a refillable spray mop container.

To Use: Dampen a microfiber mop applicator or pad with water; spray solution on floor and wipe clean. Apply in one direction and rinse microfiber floor pad frequently to avoid streaks.

To Store: Store in a sealed, airtight container for up to 1 week.

Citrus Tile Floor Cleaner

ABOUT 1 GALLON

Tile can get grungy in a hurry. Here's a great recipe that will cut the grime and leave your floors clean—no rinsing required.

¼ CUP BORAX

1 GALLON HOT WATER

5 DROPS LEMON ESSENTIAL OIL

5 DROPS ORANGE ESSENTIAL OIL

Variations:

UNSCENTED — Omit the essential oils.

EXTRA CLEANING — If your floors are extra dirty, add 1 or 2 drops of castile or dish soap to the solution. Rinsing should still not be necessary.

To Make: Mix borax, water, and essential oil in your mopping bucket. Stir to dissolve.

To Use: Mop floors as usual. Rinsing is not usually necessary.

To Store: This is a one-time-use product; no storage necessary.

HELPFUL HINT

If your floors are extra dirty, have a bucket of clean water alongside your cleaning solution. Rinse in the plain water bucket instead of the cleaning bucket—this will ensure clean water is on your floors and it should eliminate streaking.

Lemon and Mint Vinyl Floor Cleaner—Spray

ABOUT 16 OUNCES

Vinyl floors dirty and sticky? This spray dries quickly, kills germs, and will brighten up those vinyl floors pronto!

5 OUNCES WATER, DISTILLED OR BOILED AND COOLED

5 OUNCES DISTILLED WHITE VINEGAR

5 OUNCES RUBBING ALCOHOL

3 DROPS LEMON ESSENTIAL OIL

2 DROPS PEPPERMINT ESSENTIAL OIL

Variations:

UNSCENTED — Omit the essential oils.

LEMON AND CLOVE — Substitute clove essential oil for the peppermint.

To Make: Add ingredients to a spray bottle and shake to combine.

To Use: Spray on vinyl floor and mop with a wet mop or wet microfiber padded mop; continue until floor is clean.

To Store: Store in a cool, dark place for up to 1 month.

TIME-SAVING TIP

Keep this spray bottle handy to spot-clean your vinyl floors in between your weekly floor washing.

Carpet Disinfectant and Cleaner

If you have a particular icky carpet spot (stomach bug going around the house?) that needs to be disinfected, try this solution. I prefer vodka because there's virtually no smell and it seems to absorb any odors a little better.

VODKA OR RUBBING ALCOHOL

To Make: Pour vodka or rubbing alcohol on the stain or spot.

To Use: Blot stain or spill (never rub a stain, it will only set it) with clean white cloths or paper towels. Repeat as necessary.

To Store: Vodka and alcohol will last indefinitely.

Carpet Spot Remover (Unknown Spot)

I have carpet stain removal on my rotating cleaning list because I don't always catch stains right away. I go through my house and check for any stains and apply this simple solution to rid my home of any unknown stains.

ENOUGH DISTILLED WHITE VINEGAR TO COVER STAIN

BAKING SODA

To Make: Cover the stain with the white vinegar. Sprinkle baking soda on top of the vinegar. The stain will bubble up from the carpet.

To Use: Let the baking soda sit on the carpet until it is dry. This can take a day or two, so you may want to cover the spot with a towel, container, or bowl to keep it contained. Vacuum up the residue.

To Store: This is a one-time-use product; no storage necessary.

Carpet Stain Remover

If you catch a carpet stain early, you can generally get the stain removed, and without nasty chemicals. Take care to blot and not rub the stain, as rubbing will ruin the carpet fibers.

4 CUPS WARM WATER, DIVIDED

½ TEASPOON CLEAR CASTILE SOAP OR DISH SOAP

Variation:

PET ODOR NEUTRALIZER — Once you have successfully cleaned the spot, sprinkle the area with baking soda to neutralize any odors left behind. A pet is more likely to return to its "spot" (and leave you *another* stain) if there is any scent left behind. Cover the spot so a pet or small child doesn't disturb the baking soda. Let sit and dry overnight and vacuum up the residue.

To Make: Mix a solution of 2 cups warm water and ½ teaspoon clear dishwashing soap. Have an additional container with 2 cups of plain warm water handy for rinsing.

To Use: Soak a clean rag or paper towel in the mixture, wring out, and gently blot the stain with it. After you have blotted with the soap solution, use a clean rag soaked in warm water to remove the residue. Alternate the soap solution with the fresh water until the stain is gone.

To Store: This is a one-time-use product; no storage necessary.

Carpet Cleaner for Machines

1 GALLON, OR ENOUGH TO FILL 1 CARPET-CLEANING MACHINE

This recipe was recommended to me by a carpet-cleaning professional. It's easy to mix and use, and doesn't suds up or leave any residue behind. Refer to your carpet-cleaning machine's detergent capacity for the exact liquid amounts. Most carpet cleaners can hold about a gallon to a gallon and a half of liquid.

4 CUPS HOT WATER

4 CUPS DISTILLED WHITE VINEGAR

10–15 DROPS LEMON ESSENTIAL OIL
(to minimize the vinegar scent)

Variation:

UNSCENTED — Omit the essential oil.

To Make: Pour liquids into liquid dispenser.

To Use: Run carpet cleaner as usual. Any vinegar scent will dissipate as soon as the carpets are dry.

To Store: This is a one-time-use product; no storage necessary.

MONEY-SAVING TIP

Cleaning your own carpets can save you hundreds of dollars, and using vinegar and water as your cleaning solution will save you even more money. You can rent a carpet cleaner by the day, or you may choose to purchase one, once you see how easy it is to make your own effective cleaners for your machine.

Citrus and Mint Hardwood Floor Cleaner—Bucket

ABOUT 1 GALLON

Hardwood floors are beautiful—but they're especially breathtaking when they are clean. This recipe smells amazing and the floors look even better! Make sure that you use a barely damp sponge or cloth when you are washing your floors—standing water can damage hardwoods.

1 GALLON WARM WATER

½ CUP DISTILLED WHITE VINEGAR

3 DROPS LEMON OR ORANGE ESSENTIAL OIL

2 DROPS PEPPERMINT ESSENTIAL OIL

Variation:

LEMON AND CLOVE — Use 3 drops lemon essential oil and substitute 2 drops clove for the peppermint.

To Make: Mix water, vinegar, and oils in a large bucket or container.

To Use: Mop with a dry mop and bucket or by hand with microfiber cloths. Rinse often and change solution as needed during cleaning.

To Store: This is a one-time-use product; no storage necessary.

HELPFUL HINT

Vinegar does have a pH and is considered a mild acid, so you want to make sure that you are following the ratio of 1 part vinegar : 32 parts water when making a hardwood floor cleaning solution.

Lemon and Clove Hardwood Floor Cleaner—Spray Mop

ABOUT 16 OUNCES

If you love the ease and convenience of a refillable spray mop, you'll fall head over heels for this recipe.

16 OUNCES WARM WATER, DISTILLED OR BOILED AND COOLED

3 TEASPOONS DISTILLED WHITE VINEGAR

1 DROP LEMON ESSENTIAL OIL

1 DROP CLOVE ESSENTIAL OIL

Variation:

CITRUS AND MINT—Use 1 drop of lemon or orange essential oil and 1 drop of peppermint instead of the clove.

To Make: Pour ingredients in spray mop dispenser.

To Use: Dampen mop pad with warm water. Spray solution on floor, then mop it up, taking care to wipe solution immediately after spraying on floor.

To Store: Store in the dispenser for up to 1 month.

MONEY-SAVING TIP

Look for a refillable spray mop with washable microfiber pads. The pads can be washed at least 300 times—talk about a money saver!

pH-Neutral Hardwood Floor Cleaner

1 PH-NEUTRALLY CLEANED FLOOR

If you're concerned about using vinegar on your hardwood floors, take the pH-neutral approach and just use warm water. A microfiber cloth and warm water will clean most "everyday" dirt on your wood floors. Add a little essential oil to make the job more enjoyable.

WARM WATER

2 DROPS ESSENTIAL OIL

To Make: Use a bucket and spray mop or microfiber dusting mop.

To Use: Fill a bucket with warm water and add 2 drops of your favorite essential oil (lemon is great for this purpose). Spray or dip and mop. Take care to not allow any water to stand on your hardwood floor, as this can quickly damage your hardwoods.

To Store: This is a one-time-use product; no storage necessary.

Floor Wipes—Dry

···

Disposable floor sweepers are great for trapping dust, fur, hair, and dirt. If you want to try to make your own, look no further than the automotive aisle for your microfiber cloths. You'll find a big pack of microfiber cloths that you can repurpose for just about any cleaning task around the home. I love them for floor wipes because they tend to be a little larger than the standard size so they work really well over your floor mop head.

1 PACKAGE OF MICROFIBER CLEANING CLOTHS—at least 12" × 16"

Variation:

SCENTED—Put a drop of essential oil on the wipe before placing on the sweeper for instant scented floor wipes. Lavender, lemon, orange? Any scent that gets you in the floor-sweeping mood.

To Make: Fit microfiber cloths over floor sweeper—pinch fabric into place.

To Use: Once cloth is secured in floor sweeper, simply push over your floor, picking up any dirt. Launder used rags with the rest of your cleaning rags.

To Store: Store indefinitely.

HELPFUL HINT

Flip the cloth over and use the other side before laundering. First shake any dirt or dust out in the garbage or outside if necessary.

Floor Wipes—Wet

Love the convenience of floor wipes, but not the cost? These reusable wipes will have you singing their praises. They'll keep for a week, so try to gauge how many you'll need—you never know, it might be an 8-floor-wipe kind of week . . .

1 PACKAGE OF MICROFIBER CLEANING CLOTHS—at least 12" × 16"

16 OUNCES WATER, DISTILLED OR BOILED AND COOLED

3 TEASPOONS DISTILLED WHITE VINEGAR

2 DROPS ESSENTIAL OIL, SUCH AS LEMON, ORANGE, OR TEA TREE

To Make: Mix water, vinegar and essential oil together. Place cloths in large container with a lid. A 2-cup wide-mouth canning jar will work with up to 6 or 7 cleaning cloths. Pour liquid over cloths. Place lid on container; swirl and mix to make sure liquid has been absorbed into cloths. Leaving about a cup behind, pour excess liquid out of container.

To Use: Place microfiber cloth over floor sweeper—pinch fabric into place. Wipe floors with cloth. Replace as needed. One cloth should be enough for a small room. Launder as usual.

To Store: Store in container for up to 1 week.

Baseboard and Door Cleaner

I have white painted doors and trim in my home, so cute little handprints show up quickly. This is my go-to cleaning solution for baseboards and doors in my home.

½ CUP BORAX

1 GALLON WARM WATER

To Make: Dissolve borax in warm water; stir to combine.

To Use: Dip microfiber cloth or sponge in solution. Wring out any excess water, and wipe baseboards and/or doors to clean. No rinsing is necessary.

To Store: This is a one-time-use product; no storage necessary.

HELPFUL HINT

Keep old bath towels nearby to place under bucket and to catch any drips. Wash doors from top to bottom and left to right.

CHAPTER 8

RECIPES FOR THE NURSERY AND PLAYROOM

If you have young children, you'll love these natural and safe recipes. Isn't it amazing that as soon as baby starts crawling and putting anything that fits into his or her mouth, everything seems so much dirtier? Try your hand at these simple solutions for your little ones' playspaces and toys. The best part is that they are so simple to make. That's key for busy parents—I'm guessing that you don't have a spare minute to be concocting cleaning recipes. You'll find that these recipes are easy to make, have a simple scent or no scent, and use lots of vegetable-based soap and water for a clean baby and a happy mama.

Citrus and Tea Tree Fabric Sanitizer Spray

12 OUNCES

Sometimes you just need to give that fabric a spray to make sure it's really clean. Use this formula on fabrics that aren't machine washable or that you don't have time right now to launder. Did baby spit up on a chair or on your fabric changing-table cover? Give it a little spritz until you can really wash it.

8 OUNCES WATER, DISTILLED OR BOILED AND COOLED

4 OUNCES VODKA OR RUBBING ALCOHOL

2 DROPS ORANGE ESSENTIAL OIL

4 DROPS TEA TREE ESSENTIAL OIL

To Make: Add ingredients to a spray bottle and shake to combine.

To Use: Spray very lightly on fabric that needs to be sanitized or freshened a bit. Allow to thoroughly dry before using fabric.

To Store: Store for up to 2 months.

Citrus Diaper Pail Fresheners

If you have a diaper pail, you need these fresheners. Put a few of them in a small canning jar with a cute label, wrap up some diapers, and give to a new mom!

1 CUP BAKING SODA

¾ CUP EPSOM SALTS

ABOUT ½ CUP WATER

10 DROPS ESSENTIAL OIL—any combination of lemon, lime, orange, or grapefruit is great in this recipe

ICE CUBE TRAY(S)

To Make: Combine soda and Epsom salts and add essential oils. Slowly stir in water to make a dry paste. Spoon about a tablespoon in each compartment of an ice cube tray, packing down tightly and about ¾ full. This combination will expand a little. Allow to dry out and completely harden overnight or in the sun. Once the tablets have hardened, carefully turn the tray over onto a clean surface. The tablets should fall out without any twisting or banging, which could break them into pieces.

To Use: Place 1 or 2 fresheners in your diaper pail or garbage can. Each freshener will freshen for at least 2 weeks.

To Store: Store in an airtight container for up to 3 months.

Hand Sanitizer Spray

2 OUNCES

Prefer a liquid spray for your hand sanitizing needs? Ditch the mall-brand chemical version and try this. Keep it in your purse for a quick spritz. The witch hazel is a natural astringent but the vitamin E will help moisturize.

2 OUNCES WITCH HAZEL

1 TEASPOON VITAMIN E OIL

5 DROPS TEA TREE ESSENTIAL OIL

2 DROPS LEMON ESSENTIAL OIL

Variation:

LAVENDER — Substitute lavender essential oil for the lemon.

To Make: Dispense ingredients directly into a small container with a spray top and shake to combine.

To Use: Squirt on hands, rub thoroughly, and allow to air-dry.

To Store: Keep out of the reach of small children, but store where you'll use it most—purse, nursery, or car. Will keep for 2 months.

Hand Sanitizer Gel

This is my kids' favorite hand sanitizer recipe. It cleans, leaves hands soft, and is safe for the kids to use themselves.

1½ OUNCES PURE ALOE VERA (not the green stuff)

3 TEASPOONS RUBBING ALCOHOL

1 TEASPOON VITAMIN E OIL

5 DROPS PEPPERMINT ESSENTIAL OIL

Variations:

UNSCENTED — Omit the essential oil.

CITRUS — Substitute lemon or orange essential oil for the peppermint.

To Make: Dispense ingredients directly into a small container with a lid. Shake liberally to mix all ingredients thoroughly. If you want your gel to be slightly thinner in consistency, add an additional teaspoon of rubbing alcohol.

To Use: Squirt on hands, rub thoroughly, and allow to air-dry.

To Store: Keep out of the reach of small children, but store where you'll use it most—purse, nursery, or car. Will keep for 2 months.

Lemon Room-Freshening Spray

12 OUNCES

Keep this spray handy for any time a room needs a little spritz of something to freshen it up after the kids have made it smelly!

1 CUP WATER, DISTILLED OR BOILED AND COOLED

½ CUP VODKA

10–20 DROPS LEMON ESSENTIAL OIL—put in 10 drops and give it a spray. Add more essential oil to your liking if needed.

Variation:

LAVENDER AND MINT—Substitute 5 drops lavender and 5 drops peppermint essential oil for the lemon—adjust to your liking.

To Make: Add ingredients to a spray bottle and shake to combine.

To Use: Spray 2 or 3 sprays in any room that needs freshening.

To Store: Store in a cool place for up to 2 months.

Toy Cleaner—Soak

....

1 PLAYROOMFUL OF CLEAN TOYS

If you've had a bout of sickness run through your house or just want to give the toys a little bath, this is an easy way to do it.

1 TABLESPOON LIQUID CASTILE SOAP, CITRUS OR UNSCENTED

SINK WITH WARM WATER

To Make: Fill sink with water and castile soap. Have a clean, dry towel ready to set toys to air-dry.

To Use: Wash, rinse, and dry toys. Let them air-dry on the counter, or set out in the sun to get a little free sun sanitizing.

To Store: This is a one-time-use product; no storage necessary.

KID-FRIENDLY TIP

My kids love to stand on a chair at the sink and give their plastic toys a bath. Fill the sink and let them scrub and rinse their own toys. It's a cleaning win in my book.

Toy Cleaner—Spray

8 OUNCES

If you'd like a toy cleaner in spray form, here's a great natural solution. Keep the bottle out of reach of children, but it's safe to use around them.

4 OUNCES WATER, DISTILLED OR BOILED AND COOLED

4 OUNCES WHITE VINEGAR

2 DROPS LEMON ESSENTIAL OIL

To Make: Mix ingredients in spray bottle and shake to combine.

To Use: Spray on toys. Rinse if toys will be in child's mouth or if desired. Air-dry.

To Store: Store in spray bottle for up to 2 months.

KID-FRIENDLY TIP

You can also use straight hydrogen peroxide (3 percent) to sanitize kids' toys and surfaces. Place a spray top on a hydrogen peroxide bottle and spray any offending toys. Let hydrogen peroxide dry and rinse in warm water. Allow to air-dry.

Bathtub Toy Cleaner

1 SET OF CLEAN BATHTUB TOYS

Bathtub toys can be a breeding ground for bacteria and mold. Look for toys that don't have holes in the bottom to keep the bacteria and mold to a minimum. My kids love measuring cups, bowls, and colanders. Give your bath toys a bath in the dishwasher monthly to rid them of mold and bacteria.

1 LEMON DISHWASHER DETERGENT TABLET (see Chapter 3)

To Make: Place bathtub toys on the top rack of dishwasher and run a cleaning cycle with the tablet.

To Use: Wash toys and allow to air-dry on the counter or outside in the sun.

To Store: This is a one-time-use product; no storage necessary.

Baby Stain Spray Remover

8 OUNCES

Babies spit up a lot, but stains don't always come out in the first laundering—especially if you are too exhausted to remember to pretreat. This simple spray will help get those stains out once and for all.

8 OUNCES WATER, DISTILLED OR BOILED AND SLIGHTLY COOLED

2 TABLESPOONS BORAX

2 TABLESPOONS LEMON AND LAVENDER LIQUID LAUNDRY SOAP
(see Chapter 5)

To Make: Add borax and laundry detergent to a spray bottle and pour warm water over the borax. Shake thoroughly to combine.

To Use: Spray directly on stain and toss in the washer.

To Store: Store in spray bottle for up to 1 month.

Cloth Diaper Soak

1 LOAD OF CLEAN DIAPERS

If you use cloth diapers, you need a diaper soak in your laundry room. Here's a super-simple soak that you can do for a few hours or overnight. The borax acts as a laundry booster and deodorizer in this recipe.

½–1 CUP BORAX

½ CUP LEMON AND LAVENDER LIQUID LAUNDRY SOAP (see Chapter 5)

To Make: Fill washing machine with dirty diapers, hot water, laundry detergent, and borax. If you have an HE machine, put the borax in with your detergent.

To Use: Wash and set the machine to soak for a few hours or overnight. Launder as usual.

To Store: This is a one-time-use product; no storage necessary.

Bleach Alternative

Bleach can be irritating to babies' skin (and adults' too), but there are times when a whitener is needed. Here's a great formula to add in with your detergent.

2 OUNCES OR ¼ CUP HYDROGEN PEROXIDE

To Make: Add this to the bleach compartment on your HE washing machine, or directly to the water if you have a regular machine.

To Use: Launder as usual. Make sure that you are treating hydrogen peroxide like bleach and not using it anywhere near your brights or colors.

To Store: Keep a bottle of hydrogen peroxide in your laundry room if you have lots of whites to whiten.

Kids' Cleaning Wipes

It's a great idea to get kids involved in cleaning up after themselves, but handing a toxic wipe to them just doesn't seem right. A kids' cleaning wipe that works and is safe for them to use? That's what I need!

12 THICK AND DURABLE PAPER TOWELS (such as Bounty DuraTowels)

2 CUPS WATER (boiled and cooled or distilled if storing for longer than a couple of days)

1 TABLESPOON CASTILE SOAP

To Make: Tear off about a dozen paper towels, cut them in half, and stack into a neat pile. Roll up the paper towels and stuff them in a 2-cup, wide-mouth mason jar. Mix the ingredients in a large measuring cup and pour over the paper towels in the mason jar. Put the lid on and shake and swirl the liquid around to make sure that it is absorbed into the paper towels. (A large zip-top bag or baby wipe container also works for storing these wipes if you don't have a mason jar—the bag will save space as well.)

To Use: Pour off all excess liquid in the container before using to ensure a less wet wipe. Let helpful kids use these to wipe down doors, windowsills, baseboards, tables, counters, and other areas that need a little cleaning swipe.

To Store: Store in a sealed, airtight container for up to 1 week.

Lemon and Mint Hand and Face Wipes

If you've ever thought about the chemicals you are putting on your (or your kids') hands and face when you use a commercial hand or face wipe, it might be time to switch to a natural version. You'll love the refreshing scent of lemon and mint—and the nontoxic ingredients!

12 THICK AND DURABLE PAPER TOWELS
(such as Bounty DuraTowels)

2 CUPS WATER (boiled and cooled or distilled if storing for longer than a couple of days)

1 TABLESPOON WITCH HAZEL

1 TABLESPOON CITRUS CASTILE SOAP

1 TABLESPOON FRACTIONATED COCONUT OIL OR ALMOND OIL

5 DROPS LEMON ESSENTIAL OIL

2 DROPS PEPPERMINT ESSENTIAL OIL

Variations:

UNSCENTED — Use unscented castile soap and don't add any essential oils.

CITRUS — Add lime, grapefruit, or orange essential oil instead of the peppermint.

To Make: Tear off about a dozen paper towels, cut them in half, and stack into a neat pile. Roll up the paper towels and stuff them in a 2-cup, wide-mouth mason jar. Mix the ingredients in a large measuring cup and pour over the paper towels in the mason jar. Put the lid on and shake and swirl the liquid around to make sure that it is absorbed into the paper towels. (A large zip-top bag also works for storing these wipes if you don't have a mason jar—the bag will save space as well.)

To Use: Just pull a wipe up from the center, wipe hands, and air-dry.

To Store: Store in a sealed, airtight container for up to 1 week.

TIME-SAVING TIP

I love making a batch of wipes for picnics and park trips, but rarely have time the morning of an event to whip up a batch. Instead, I keep precut paper towels in a large zip-top bag in the pantry, so I don't have to cut them at the last minute. If you want to be even more efficient, you could have a couple of mason jars in your pantry with paper towels cut and rolled and inserted in the jars. The best thing about these wipes is that I know that my kids' hands are clean and I also know what they cleaned them with. I keep a little more of the liquid in the jar because I like the wipes to have plenty of solution on them. Adjust for your personal preference.

CHAPTER 9

RECIPES FOR THE GARAGE/BASEMENT/ GARDEN

Keeping the outside spaces clean and tidy can be difficult to manage with all the forces at work on them—dirt, mud, leaves, rain, and so on. The basement has its share of problems with dampness and odors. With the recipes in this chapter, you'll be able to clean your grill, patio, or porch and maintain your furnace and dehumidifier with ease and expertise. Here are my favorite recipes and techniques to organically keep the outside of my home just as clean as the inside.

Garden Tool Cleaning Kit

You should clean garden tools after each use, but that's tough to do when you're exhausted after a long day of planting or weeding. At the beginning or the end of the garden season, try to give your tools a little bath.

5-GALLON BUCKET
WARM WATER
1 TABLESPOON CASTILE SOAP
5 DROPS ROSEMARY ESSENTIAL OIL

To Make: Combine water and soap in large bucket.

To Use: Soak tools for a few minutes, scrub with a scrub brush, and dry thoroughly. Oil any tools if necessary.

To Store: This is a one-time-use product; no storage necessary.

HELPFUL HINT

You can store your tools in a large garden pot with play sand in it. Add 1 or 2 tablespoons of mineral oil if you'd like and stir it into the sand to help lubricate the tools. This keeps the mechanisms running smoothly and keeps the rust away.

Cement Patio and Pavers

1 CLEAN PATIO

Most patios can be effectively cleaned with a pressure washer and warm water, but if you don't have one, or want a little more brightening power, try this recipe.

1 GALLON WARM WATER

2 TABLESPOONS HOMEMADE OXYGEN BLEACH PASTE (SEE CHAPTER 5)

To Make: Mix warm water and Oxygen Bleach Paste in large bucket. Mix to combine.

To Use: Mop or brush cement in sections and rinse thoroughly. Repeat in areas as necessary.

To Store: This is a one-time-use product; no storage necessary.

Deck—Composite and Wood

1 SUPER-CLEAN DECK

Cleaning your deck before or after a season is necessary to remove any mold or mildew that's grown. Try this two-ingredient solution the next time your deck needs a little cleaning.

1 GALLON WARM WATER

1–2 CUPS DISTILLED WHITE VINEGAR—less for just a simple cleaning and more for a deep cleaning

To Make: Mix water and vinegar in a large bucket.

To Use: Thoroughly wet deck with your hose and water first. Using a sturdy mop or broom, scrub the vinegar water solution in sections to clean. Rinse thoroughly.

To Store: This is a one-time-use product; no storage necessary.

HELPFUL HINT

Use a sponge and this same solution to wash spindles and railings on your deck.

Deck and Patio Furniture

If you have deck furniture, you probably eat outside and need to give your outside furniture a good washing from time to time. This simple soapy solution works for just about any deck furniture. Just mix, apply, and rinse. No need to dry with a towel, just air-dry.

16 OUNCES WARM WATER

2 TABLESPOONS CASTILE SOAP

2 DROPS ORANGE ESSENTIAL OIL

Variation:

UNSCENTED — Use unscented castile soap and don't add any essential oil.

To Make: Add ingredients to a spray bottle and shake to combine.

To Use: Wet furniture with hose, spray with soapy solution, rinse, and air-dry.

To Store: Store indefinitely.

Paintbrush Cleaner

....

1 CUP—enough to clean 6 paintbrushes

We've all done it: Finished a project and washed out the paintbrushes too quickly only to come back the next day to hard and crusty paintbrushes. This super-easy and natural solution will soften your paintbrushes in a hurry.

1 CUP HOT VINEGAR

1 TABLESPOON CASTILE SOAP

To Make: Heat vinegar in a microwave-safe container. Place paintbrush or paintbrushes (bristles only) in vinegar for at least an hour to overnight to soak and dissolve the paint.

To Use: Once paintbrushes have soaked in solution, rinse, and repeat if necessary. Apply tablespoon of castile soap and wash thoroughly. Dry excess water with a clean cloth or paper towel and set in the sun or outside to continue drying.

To Store: This is a one-time-use product; no storage necessary.

TIME-SAVING TIP

The next time you have a painting project, use this cleaning solution the first time, and you'll eliminate the hard, crunchy brushes.

Heavy-Duty Window Cleaner

If you're brave enough to wash the outside of your windows, you need a high-powered cleaner. Mix up this solution and use a squeegee for a professional look.

½ GALLON OR 64 OUNCES WARM WATER

4 TABLESPOONS RUBBING ALCOHOL

4 TABLESPOONS SCENTED CASTILE SOAP, SUCH AS PEPPERMINT

Variation:

SPRAY BOTTLE — You can mix this up in a small batch and use it inside as well. Pour 16 ounces of warm water in a spray bottle and add 1 tablespoon of castile soap and 1 tablespoon of rubbing alcohol. Shake to combine. Spray and wipe or squeegee clean.

To Make: Add warm water, alcohol, and castile soap to bucket. Stir to combine.

To Use: Use a squeegee with a sponge attachment to scrub bugs and dirt away. Squeegee the solution away and wipe up excess. If windows are high, you can also spray with water to rinse and clean.

To Store: This is a one-time-use product; no storage necessary.

Heavy-Duty Floor Cleaner

1 GALLON

Garage and basement floors take a beating. Try this simple and nontoxic solution to cut grease and grime and get those surfaces back to normal.

1 GALLON WARM WATER
1 CUP DISTILLED WHITE VINEGAR
¼ CUP BORAX

Variation:

DISINFECTING — Add 5 to 10 drops tea tree essential oil to the solution to up the germ-killing benefits.

To Make: Mix all ingredients in a bucket.

To Use: Mop, rinse, and allow to air-dry.

To Store: This is a one-time-use product; no storage necessary.

Outside Toy Cleaner

. . . .

1 SET OF CLEAN OUTSIDE TOYS

If you keep plastic toys outside, they probably get a little dirty from time to time. Here's an easy way to clean them naturally.

1 CUP WATER, DISTILLED OR BOILED AND COOLED

1 CUP WHITE VINEGAR

To Make: Add ingredients to a spray bottle and shake to combine.

To Use: Spray thoroughly on toys. Rinse with hose and air-dry.

To Store: Store for up to 2 months in spray bottle.

HELPFUL HINT

Use your homemade melamine sponges (see the recipe for Soap Scum Sponges in Chapter 4) to get rid of big and little stains on outside plastic toys and furniture.

Humidifier and Dehumidifier Cleaner

Did you know that you should clean regularly used humidifiers and dehumidifiers weekly, or at least monthly? Thankfully, it's a pretty easy process so you can add it to your cleaning task list.

DISTILLED WHITE VINEGAR

Variation:

DISINFECTING—For a little extra germ-killing, wipe hydrogen peroxide on the outside and inside of the humidifier or dehumidifier after you have cleaned it.

To Make: This cleaning process will depend on your machine, but for the most part, all machines can be cleaned with white vinegar and a scrub brush, followed by a thorough rinse.

To Use: Unplug and empty machine of water. Disassemble any parts that can be disassembled. Fill base with white vinegar—about a cup. Let sit and soak; cover and shake a bit to evenly distribute the vinegar. Wipe any exposed parts with vinegar on a cleaning cloth or paper towel. Rinse thoroughly, let dry, and reassemble.

To Store: This is a one-time-use product; no storage necessary.

HELPFUL HINT

Always use distilled water in your humidifier to prevent extra unnecessary mineral build-up from your water.

Air Filter—Furnace

1 CLEAN FURNACE FILTER

Did you know that you should replace your furnace filter monthly? Some filters have a 3-month lifespan, but replacing your filters on a regular basis will cut down on dust and allergens in the air. It's important to also keep the area around the furnace clean and dust-free. Next time it's time to replace your filter, bring your vacuum cleaner along to your furnace.

VACUUM

To Make: If you have replaceable furnace filters, jot down the size and go to the store and get what you need. Buy extra so you don't have to do this again next month.

To Use: Turn off furnace. Vacuum around area and remove old furnace filter. Bring a plastic garbage bag with you to contain the icky filter upon removal. Vacuum area where old filter was and put new filter in its place. If you have a washable furnace filter, bring it outside and give it a hosing down, and let it dry in the sun if possible.

To Store: Store your furnace filters near your furnace so you aren't searching for them next month.

Car Washing Solution

Remember the days of washing the car with a big soapy bucket and giant sponge? Those days are here again with this easy solution. Use microfiber cloths for a streak-free shine!

WARM WATER

1–2 TABLESPOONS CASTILE SOAP—
unscented or scented

To Make: Fill large (e.g., 5-gallon) bucket with warm or hot water and castile soap.

To Use: Use hose and wet your car. Dip sponge or cloth in water and start scrubbing. Rinse and dry thoroughly.

To Store: This is a one-time-use product; no storage necessary.

KID-FRIENDLY TIP

Get the whole family involved with a few extra sponges. Washing your car is fun again!

Car Interior Wipes

Using a spray bottle in the car can lead to spots on windows and upholstery. Try these minty wipes to clean the leather, plastic, and faux leather in your car.

12 THICK AND DURABLE PAPER TOWELS (such as Bounty DuraTowels)

3 TABLESPOONS ALMOND OIL

½ CUP VINEGAR

¾ CUP WATER, DISTILLED OR BOILED AND COOLED

2 DROPS PEPPERMINT ESSENTIAL OIL

To Make: Tear off about a dozen paper towels, cut them in half, and stack into a neat pile. Roll up the paper towels and stuff them in a 2-cup, wide-mouth mason jar. Mix the ingredients in a large measuring cup and pour over the paper towels in the mason jar. Put the lid on and shake and swirl the liquid around to make sure that it is absorbed into the paper towels. Pour off excess, as this wipe works better a little on the dry side. (A large zip-top bag or baby wipe container also works for storing these wipes if you don't have a mason jar—the bag will save space as well.)

To Use: Carefully remove a wipe or two, wring out any excess cleaner, and use as you would any cleaning wipe.

To Store: Store in a sealed, airtight container for up to 1 week.

Grill Cleaner

．．．

1 CLEAN GRILL

Grills get greasy and dirty quickly, and that mess can affect the flavor of your food. Here are a couple of easy ways to clean them from the inside out.

1 CUP WARM WATER
DISTILLED WHITE VINEGAR
¼–½ CUP BAKING SODA

To Make: Mix a paste of baking soda and water.

To Use: Open up cool grill and apply paste to the grates. Close lid and apply white vinegar to cleaning cloth or paper towels. Wipe the exterior of your grill with the vinegar. (No rinsing is necessary.) After exterior is clean, remove grates and scrub in sink or outside with a brush. Rinse thoroughly and return grates to grill. Keep grill open to allow the grates to dry completely.

To Store: This is a one-time-use product; no storage necessary.

HELPFUL HINT

After every grilling session, keep the grill on for a bit to burn off and scrape any remaining food particles. This will keep your grill cleaner in between meals.

Natural Insect Repellent

You see a lot of debate in the news about whether commercial insect repellents are safe to use. Here's a simple recipe that keeps insects away and is safe to use around your family. The oils listed in this recipe are known for their fly-, tick-, and flea-repelling properties.

4 OUNCES WITCH HAZEL OR VODKA

2 TEASPOONS ALMOND OIL

10 DROPS ESSENTIAL OILS—combine 3 of these oils: lemon, lemongrass, citronella, peppermint, lavender, cedar

To Make: Pour ingredients in small spray bottle or container.

To Use: Spray on hands and rub hands together. Dab around areas where bugs and flies are bothering you. Be careful to not spray directly on clothes, as the oil may stain.

To Store: Store for up to 2 months in a cool place.

CLEANING CHECKLISTS

Weekly Cleaning Checklist

MONDAY ☐

- ☐ CLEAN BATHROOMS
- ☐ SWEEP FLOORS
- ☐ WIPE COUNTERS
- ☐ DECLUTTER
- ☐ DO A LOAD OF LAUNDRY

- ☐ _____
- ☐ _____
- ☐ _____
- ☐ _____
- ☐ _____

TUESDAY ☐

- ☐ DUST HOUSE
- ☐ SWEEP FLOORS
- ☐ WIPE COUNTERS
- ☐ DECLUTTER
- ☐ DO A LOAD OF LAUNDRY

- ☐ _____
- ☐ _____
- ☐ _____
- ☐ _____
- ☐ _____

WEDNESDAY ☐

- ☐ VACUUM FLOORS
- ☐ SWEEP FLOORS
- ☐ WIPE COUNTERS
- ☐ DECLUTTER
- ☐ DO A LOAD OF LAUNDRY

- ☐ _____
- ☐ _____
- ☐ _____
- ☐ _____
- ☐ _____

THURSDAY ☐

- ☐ WASH ALL FLOORS
- ☐ SWEEP FLOORS
- ☐ WIPE COUNTERS
- ☐ DECLUTTER
- ☐ DO A LOAD OF LAUNDRY

- ☐ _____
- ☐ _____
- ☐ _____
- ☐ _____
- ☐ _____

FRIDAY ☐

- ☐ CATCH-UP DAY
- ☐ SWEEP FLOORS
- ☐ WIPE COUNTERS
- ☐ DECLUTTER
- ☐ DO A LOAD OF LAUNDRY

- ☐ _____
- ☐ _____
- ☐ _____
- ☐ _____
- ☐ _____

SATURDAY ☐

- ☐ WASH SHEETS ± TOWELS
- ☐ SWEEP FLOORS
- ☐ WIPE COUNTERS
- ☐ DECLUTTER
- ☐ DO A LOAD OF LAUNDRY (IF NECESSARY)

- ☐ _____
- ☐ _____
- ☐ _____
- ☐ _____
- ☐ _____

SUNDAY ☐

- ☐ SWEEP FLOORS
- ☐ WIPE COUNTERS
- ☐ DECLUTTER
- ☐ DO A LOAD OF LAUNDRY

- ☐ _____
- ☐ _____
- ☐ _____
- ☐ _____

PHONE CALLS: ☐

- ☐ _____
- ☐ _____
- ☐ _____

- ☐ _____
- ☐ _____
- ☐ _____

E-MAILS: ☐

- ☐ _____
- ☐ _____
- ☐ _____

- ☐ _____
- ☐ _____
- ☐ _____

APPOINTMENTS: ☐

- ☐ _____
- ☐ _____
- ☐ _____

- ☐ _____
- ☐ _____
- ☐ _____

NEXT WEEK: ☐

- ☐ _____
- ☐ _____
- ☐ _____

- ☐ _____
- ☐ _____
- ☐ _____

Weekly Cleaning Checklist (blank)

MONDAY ☐
- ☐ _____
- ☐ _____
- ☐ _____
- ☐ _____
- ☐ _____
- ☐ _____
- ☐ _____
- ☐ _____
- ☐ _____

TUESDAY ☐
- ☐ _____
- ☐ _____
- ☐ _____
- ☐ _____
- ☐ _____
- ☐ _____
- ☐ _____
- ☐ _____
- ☐ _____
- ☐ _____

WEDNESDAY ☐
- ☐ _____
- ☐ _____
- ☐ _____
- ☐ _____
- ☐ _____
- ☐ _____
- ☐ _____
- ☐ _____
- ☐ _____

THURSDAY ☐
- ☐ _____
- ☐ _____
- ☐ _____
- ☐ _____
- ☐ _____
- ☐ _____
- ☐ _____
- ☐ _____
- ☐ _____

FRIDAY ☐
- ☐ _____
- ☐ _____
- ☐ _____
- ☐ _____
- ☐ _____
- ☐ _____
- ☐ _____
- ☐ _____
- ☐ _____
- ☐ _____

SATURDAY ☐
- ☐ _____
- ☐ _____
- ☐ _____
- ☐ _____
- ☐ _____
- ☐ _____
- ☐ _____
- ☐ _____
- ☐ _____
- ☐ _____

SUNDAY ☐
- ☐ _____
- ☐ _____
- ☐ _____
- ☐ _____
- ☐ _____
- ☐ _____
- ☐ _____
- ☐ _____
- ☐ _____
- ☐ _____

PHONE CALLS: ☐
- ☐ _____
- ☐ _____
- ☐ _____
- ☐ _____
- ☐ _____
- ☐ _____

E-MAILS: ☐
- ☐ _____
- ☐ _____
- ☐ _____
- ☐ _____
- ☐ _____
- ☐ _____

APPOINTMENTS: ☐
- ☐ _____
- ☐ _____
- ☐ _____
- ☐ _____
- ☐ _____
- ☐ _____

NEXT WEEK: ☐
- ☐ _____
- ☐ _____
- ☐ _____
- ☐ _____
- ☐ _____
- ☐ _____

DOCKET FOR THE WEEK OF:

Monthly (Rotating) Cleaning Checklist

JANUARY

- [ ] VACUUM BASEBOARDS
- [ ] VACUUM ± SPOT-CLEAN FURNITURE
- [ ] CLEAN LIGHT FIXTURES IN KITCHEN
- [ ] WASH RUGS
- [ ] POLISH WOOD FURNITURE
- [ ] REPLACE FILTERS (FURNACE, HUMIDIFIERS)
- [ ] CLEAN OVEN
- [ ] WASH WINDOWS—INSIDE ± OUT
- [ ] _____

FEBRUARY

- [ ] VACUUM BASEBOARDS
- [ ] WASH BASEBOARDS
- [ ] VACUUM ± SPOT-CLEAN FURNITURE
- [ ] CLEAN LIGHT FIXTURES LIVING/DINING ROOMS
- [ ] WASH RUGS
- [ ] POLISH WOOD FURNITURE
- [ ] WIPE SWITCHES/PHONES/REMOTES
- [ ] SPOT-CLEAN WALLS
- [ ] _____

MARCH

- [ ] VACUUM BASEBOARDS
- [ ] VACUUM ± SPOT-CLEAN FURNITURE
- [ ] CLEAN LIGHT FIXTURES IN FAMILY ROOM
- [ ] WASH RUGS
- [ ] POLISH WOOD FURNITURE
- [ ] DUST CEILINGS AND CORNERS
- [ ] WASH/FLUFF PILLOWS ± BEDDING
- [ ] TURN/ROTATE/VACUUM MATTRESSES
- [ ] _____

APRIL

- [ ] VACUUM BASEBOARDS
- [ ] VACUUM ± SPOT-CLEAN FURNITURE
- [ ] CLEAN LIGHT FIXTURES IN BATHROOMS
- [ ] WASH RUGS
- [ ] POLISH WOOD FURNITURE
- [ ] CLEAN OVEN
- [ ] WIPE SWITCHES/PHONES/REMOTES
- [ ] LAUNDER DRAPERIES
- [ ] _____

MAY

- [ ] VACUUM BASEBOARDS
- [ ] WASH BASEBOARDS
- [ ] VACUUM ± SPOT-CLEAN FURNITURE
- [ ] CLEAN LIGHT FIXTURES IN MASTER BEDROOM
- [ ] WASH RUGS
- [ ] POLISH WOOD FURNITURE
- [ ] VACUUM/CLEAN WINDOW TREATMENTS
- [ ] SPOT-CLEAN WALLS
- [ ] _____

JUNE

- [ ] VACUUM BASEBOARDS
- [ ] VACUUM ± SPOT-CLEAN FURNITURE
- [ ] CLEAN LIGHT FIXTURES IN OTHER BEDROOMS
- [ ] WASH RUGS
- [ ] POLISH WOOD FURNITURE
- [ ] REPLACE FILTERS (FURNACE, HUMIDIFIERS)
- [ ] WIPE SWITCHES/PHONES/REMOTES
- [ ] WASH WINDOWS—INSIDE ± OUT
- [ ] _____

JULY

- [ ] VACUUM BASEBOARDS
- [ ] VACUUM ± SPOT-CLEAN FURNITURE
- [ ] CLEAN LIGHT FIXTURES IN KITCHEN
- [ ] WASH RUGS
- [ ] POLISH WOOD FURNITURE
- [ ] CLEAN OVEN
- [ ] DUST CEILINGS AND CORNERS
- [ ] CLEAN REFRIGERATOR/FREEZER/PANTRY
- [ ] _____

AUGUST

- [ ] VACUUM BASEBOARDS
- [ ] WASH BASEBOARDS
- [ ] VACUUM ± SPOT-CLEAN FURNITURE
- [ ] CLEAN LIGHT FIXTURES LIVING/DINING ROOMS
- [ ] WASH RUGS
- [ ] POLISH WOOD FURNITURE
- [ ] WIPE SWITCHES/PHONES/REMOTES
- [ ] SPOT-CLEAN WALLS
- [ ] _____

SEPTEMBER

- [ ] VACUUM BASEBOARDS
- [ ] VACUUM ± SPOT-CLEAN FURNITURE
- [ ] CLEAN LIGHT FIXTURES IN FAMILY ROOM
- [ ] WASH RUGS
- [ ] POLISH WOOD FURNITURE
- [ ] VACUUM/CLEAN WINDOW TREATMENTS
- [ ] WASH/FLUFF PILLOWS ± BEDDING
- [ ] TURN/ROTATE/VACUUM MATTRESSES
- [ ] _____

OCTOBER

- [ ] VACUUM BASEBOARDS
- [ ] VACUUM ± SPOT-CLEAN FURNITURE
- [ ] CLEAN LIGHT FIXTURES IN BATHROOMS
- [ ] WASH RUGS
- [ ] POLISH WOOD FURNITURE
- [ ] WIPE SWITCHES/PHONES/REMOTES
- [ ] VACUUM GARAGE
- [ ] VACUUM BASEMENT OR STORAGE AREA
- [ ] _____

NOVEMBER

- [ ] VACUUM BASEBOARDS
- [ ] WASH BASEBOARDS
- [ ] VACUUM ± SPOT-CLEAN FURNITURE
- [ ] CLEAN LIGHT FIXTURES IN MASTER BEDROOM
- [ ] WASH RUGS
- [ ] POLISH WOOD FURNITURE
- [ ] DUST CEILINGS AND CORNERS
- [ ] SPOT-CLEAN WALLS
- [ ] _____

DECEMBER

- [ ] VACUUM BASEBOARDS
- [ ] VACUUM ± SPOT-CLEAN FURNITURE
- [ ] CLEAN LIGHT FIXTURES IN OTHER BEDROOMS
- [ ] WASH RUGS
- [ ] POLISH WOOD FURNITURE
- [ ] WIPE SWITCHES/PHONES/REMOTES
- [ ] VACUUM/CLEAN WINDOW TREATMENTS
- [ ] VACUUM LAMP SHADES
- [ ] _____

Monthly (Rotating) Cleaning Checklist

MONTH:
- [ ] VACUUM BASEBOARDS
- [ ] VACUUM ± SPOT-CLEAN FURNITURE
- [ ] CLEAN LIGHT FIXTURES IN KITCHEN
- [ ] WASH RUGS
- [ ] POLISH WOOD FURNITURE
- [ ] REPLACE FILTERS (FURNACE, HUMIDIFIERS)
- [ ] CLEAN OVEN
- [ ] WASH WINDOWS—INSIDE ± OUT
- [ ] _____

MONTH:
- [ ] VACUUM BASEBOARDS
- [ ] VACUUM ± SPOT-CLEAN FURNITURE
- [ ] CLEAN LIGHT FIXTURES IN BATHROOMS
- [ ] WASH RUGS
- [ ] POLISH WOOD FURNITURE
- [ ] CLEAN OVEN
- [ ] WIPE SWITCHES/PHONES/REMOTES
- [ ] LAUNDER DRAPERIES
- [ ] _____

MONTH:
- [ ] VACUUM BASEBOARDS
- [ ] WASH BASEBOARDS
- [ ] VACUUM ± SPOT-CLEAN FURNITURE
- [ ] CLEAN LIGHT FIXTURES LIVING/DINING ROOMS
- [ ] WASH RUGS
- [ ] POLISH WOOD FURNITURE
- [ ] WIPE SWITCHES/PHONES/REMOTES
- [ ] SPOT-CLEAN WALLS
- [ ] _____

MONTH:
- [ ] VACUUM BASEBOARDS
- [ ] WASH BASEBOARDS
- [ ] VACUUM ± SPOT-CLEAN FURNITURE
- [ ] CLEAN LIGHT FIXTURES IN MASTER BEDROOM
- [ ] WASH RUGS
- [ ] POLISH WOOD FURNITURE
- [ ] VACUUM/CLEAN WINDOW TREATMENTS
- [ ] SPOT-CLEAN WALLS
- [ ] _____

MONTH:
- [ ] VACUUM BASEBOARDS
- [ ] VACUUM ± SPOT-CLEAN FURNITURE
- [ ] CLEAN LIGHT FIXTURES IN FAMILY ROOM
- [ ] WASH RUGS
- [ ] POLISH WOOD FURNITURE
- [ ] DUST CEILINGS AND CORNERS
- [ ] WASH/FLUFF PILLOWS ± BEDDING
- [ ] TURN/ROTATE/VACUUM MATTRESSES
- [ ] _____

MONTH:
- [ ] VACUUM BASEBOARDS
- [ ] VACUUM ± SPOT-CLEAN FURNITURE
- [ ] CLEAN LIGHT FIXTURES IN OTHER BEDROOMS
- [ ] WASH RUGS
- [ ] POLISH WOOD FURNITURE
- [ ] REPLACE FILTERS (FURNACE, HUMIDIFIERS)
- [ ] WIPE SWITCHES/PHONES/REMOTES
- [ ] WASH WINDOWS—INSIDE ± OUT
- [ ] _____

MONTH:

- [ ] VACUUM BASEBOARDS
- [ ] VACUUM ± SPOT-CLEAN FURNITURE
- [ ] CLEAN LIGHT FIXTURES IN KITCHEN
- [ ] WASH RUGS
- [ ] POLISH WOOD FURNITURE
- [ ] CLEAN OVEN
- [ ] DUST CEILINGS AND CORNERS
- [ ] CLEAN REFRIGERATOR/FREEZER/PANTRY
- [ ] _____

MONTH:

- [ ] VACUUM BASEBOARDS
- [ ] VACUUM ± SPOT-CLEAN FURNITURE
- [ ] CLEAN LIGHT FIXTURES IN BATHROOMS
- [ ] WASH RUGS
- [ ] POLISH WOOD FURNITURE
- [ ] WIPE SWITCHES/PHONES/REMOTES
- [ ] VACUUM GARAGE
- [ ] VACUUM BASEMENT OR STORAGE AREA
- [ ] _____

MONTH:

- [ ] VACUUM BASEBOARDS
- [ ] WASH BASEBOARDS
- [ ] VACUUM ± SPOT-CLEAN FURNITURE
- [ ] CLEAN LIGHT FIXTURES LIVING/DINING ROOMS
- [ ] WASH RUGS
- [ ] POLISH WOOD FURNITURE
- [ ] WIPE SWITCHES/PHONES/REMOTES
- [ ] SPOT-CLEAN WALLS
- [ ] _____

MONTH:

- [ ] VACUUM BASEBOARDS
- [ ] WASH BASEBOARDS
- [ ] VACUUM ± SPOT-CLEAN FURNITURE
- [ ] CLEAN LIGHT FIXTURES IN MASTER BEDROOM
- [ ] WASH RUGS
- [ ] POLISH WOOD FURNITURE
- [ ] DUST CEILINGS AND CORNERS
- [ ] SPOT-CLEAN WALLS
- [ ] _____

MONTH:

- [ ] VACUUM BASEBOARDS
- [ ] VACUUM ± SPOT-CLEAN FURNITURE
- [ ] CLEAN LIGHT FIXTURES IN FAMILY ROOM
- [ ] WASH RUGS
- [ ] POLISH WOOD FURNITURE
- [ ] VACUUM/CLEAN WINDOW TREATMENTS
- [ ] WASH/FLUFF PILLOWS ± BEDDING
- [ ] TURN/ROTATE/VACUUM MATTRESSES
- [ ] _____

MONTH:

- [ ] VACUUM BASEBOARDS
- [ ] VACUUM ± SPOT-CLEAN FURNITURE
- [ ] CLEAN LIGHT FIXTURES IN OTHER BEDROOMS
- [ ] WASH RUGS
- [ ] POLISH WOOD FURNITURE
- [ ] WIPE SWITCHES/PHONES/REMOTES
- [ ] VACUUM/CLEAN WINDOW TREATMENTS
- [ ] VACUUM LAMP SHADES
- [ ] _____

Household Cleaning Checklist (blank)

DAILY

- ☐ _____
- ☐ _____
- ☐ _____
- ☐ _____
- ☐ _____
- ☐ _____
- ☐ _____
- ☐ _____
- ☐ _____

WEEKLY

- ☐ _____
- ☐ _____
- ☐ _____
- ☐ _____
- ☐ _____
- ☐ _____
- ☐ _____
- ☐ _____
- ☐ _____

MONTHLY

- ☐ _____
- ☐ _____
- ☐ _____
- ☐ _____
- ☐ _____
- ☐ _____
- ☐ _____
- ☐ _____

- ☐ _____
- ☐ _____
- ☐ _____
- ☐ _____
- ☐ _____
- ☐ _____
- ☐ _____
- ☐ _____

SEASONALLY

- ☐ _____
- ☐ _____
- ☐ _____
- ☐ _____
- ☐ _____
- ☐ _____
- ☐ _____
- ☐ _____

ANNUALLY

- ☐ _____
- ☐ _____
- ☐ _____
- ☐ _____
- ☐ _____
- ☐ _____
- ☐ _____
- ☐ _____

Declutter Before You Clean Checklist

You can't clean surfaces that are covered in stuff. If you're getting ready for a big clean or a whole house cleaning, use this checklist to motivate yourself to get those surfaces cleared. Write down the areas that need to be cleared, clear them, and check off your list. Move on to the next space until you've rid your home of clutter. Make sure that you clean off your home's clutter "hot spots" and try to find long-term solutions for those areas so the clutter doesn't keep coming back. For example, if dirty clothes are always in a pile by your daughter's dresser, put her hamper by the dresser instead of in the closet.

☐ SURFACES   ☐ FLOORS   ☐ HOT SPOTS

☐ ENTRYWAY	☐ _____
☐ MUDROOM	☐ _____
☐ KITCHEN	☐ _____
☐ BEDROOM(S)	☐ _____
☐ BATHROOM(S)	☐ _____
☐ LIVING SPACES	☐ _____
☐ DINING ROOM	☐ _____
☐ OFFICE/WORK SPACE	☐ _____

☐ _____
☐ _____
☐ _____
☐ _____
☐ _____
☐ _____
☐ _____
☐ _____
☐ _____

The One-Day Clean

This is for anyone who wants to tackle deep cleaning in his or her home in one day. Company coming? Fed up with the dirt? Whatever your reason, start early and finish late and you'll have a clean home in one day.

HOUSE

☐ DUST CORNERS AND EDGES
☐ VACUUM BASEBOARDS
☐ WASH WINDOWS
☐ CLEAN CARPETS
☐ WASH HARD FLOORS

KITCHEN

☐ CLEAN COUNTERS
☐ SCRUB SINK
☐ CLEAN FAUCET
☐ CLEAN CABINETS
☐ WIPE DRAWERS
☐ WIPE SWITCHPLATES
☐ STRAIGHTEN PANTRY
☐ CLEAN REFRIGERATOR
☐ CLEAN FREEZER
☐ CLEAN MICROWAVE
☐ CLEAN DISHWASHER
☐ APPLIANCE FRONTS

BATHROOMS

☐ CLEAR COUNTERS
☐ WASH COUNTERS
☐ CLEAN CABINETS
☐ CLEAN SINKS
☐ CLEAN FAUCETS
☐ CLEAN MIRRORS
☐ CLEAN TUBS
☐ CLEAN SHOWERS
☐ CLEAN TOILETS
☐ WIPE SWITCHPLATES
☐ SHOWER CURTAIN
☐ CLEAN GROUT

LIVING SPACES

☐ CLEAR SURFACES
☐ DUST SURFACES
☐ DUST MANTEL
☐ DUST SHELVES
☐ WASH BLANKETS/PILLOWS
☐ DUST SOLID FURNITURE
☐ CLEAN FURNITURE
☐ WINDOW TREATMENTS
☐ CLEAN SOFAS ± CHAIRS
☐ WIPE SWITCHPLATES
☐ DUST LAMPS ± SHADES

BEDROOMS

☐ CLEAR SURFACES
☐ DUST SURFACES
☐ FLIP/ROTATE MATTRESSES
☐ WASH BLANKETS/PILLOWS
☐ WASH BEDDING
☐ DUST SOLID FURNITURE
☐ CLEAN FURNITURE
☐ WINDOW TREATMENTS
☐ WIPE SWITCHPLATES
☐ DUST LAMPS ± SHADES
☐ CLEAN DRESSERS
☐ CLEAN NIGHTSTANDS

The Weekend Clean

Need to spread a deep cleaning out over a weekend? This plan has everything spread out for a weekend game plan, perfect for a long weekend of productivity! Enlist some help and schedule a carpet cleaning to make it a little easier.

HOUSE

- [ ] DUST CORNERS AND EDGES
- [ ] VACUUM BASEBOARDS
- [ ] WASH WINDOWS
- [ ] CLEAN CARPETS
- [ ] WASH HARD FLOORS

KITCHEN

- [ ] CLEAR AND WASH COUNTERS
- [ ] SCRUB SINK AND FAUCET
- [ ] WIPE DOWN CABINETS—INSIDE AND OUT
- [ ] WIPE DOWN DRAWERS—INSIDE AND OUT
- [ ] CLEAN APPLIANCES (REFRIGERATOR, STOVE, MICROWAVE…)

BATHROOMS

- [ ] CLEAR AND WASH COUNTERS
- [ ] WIPE DOWN CABINETS—INSIDE AND OUT
- [ ] CLEAN SINKS, FIXTURES, AND MIRRORS
- [ ] CLEAN TUBS AND SHOWERS
- [ ] CLEAN TOILETS—INSIDE, OUTSIDE, AND DOWN TO THE FLOOR

LIVING SPACES

- [ ] WASH BLANKETS AND PILLOWS
- [ ] DUST FURNITURE
- [ ] POLISH FURNITURE
- [ ] STRAIGHTEN SHELVES, DISPLAYS, MANTEL
- [ ] CLEAN SOFAS AND CHAIRS

BEDROOMS

- [ ] DUST FURNITURE
- [ ] POLISH FURNITURE
- [ ] ROTATE MATTRESSES
- [ ] WASH BEDDING AND PILLOWS
- [ ] DUST LAMPS AND LAMPSHADES

The One-Week Deep Clean

If you want to get your whole house clean from top to bottom, but need to work on it in segments and spread it out over the course of a week, here's your list. Capitalize on naptimes or evenings after work for a whole week and you'll have a clean house.

SUNDAY

- [ ] DUST CORNERS AND EDGES (WALLS)
- [ ] DUST LIGHT FIXTURES
- [ ] CLEAN KITCHEN APPLIANCES
- [ ] CLEAR ± WIPE DOWN COUNTERS
- [ ] CLEAN PANTRY OR FOOD STORAGE
- [ ] CLEAN CABINET FRONTS

MONDAY

- [ ] VACUUM CORNERS AND EDGES (FLOORS)
- [ ] VACUUM BASEBOARDS
- [ ] WASH BASEBOARDS
- [ ] WASH DOORS

TUESDAY

- [ ] WIPE ALL SWITCHPLATES
- [ ] WIPE DOWN ELECTRONICS—PHONES, COMPUTERS
- [ ] VACUUM OR WASH VENT COVERS
- [ ] CLEAN SOFAS AND CHAIRS

WEDNESDAY

- [ ] CLEAN CARPETS
- [ ] CLEAR SURFACES IN LIVING AREAS—WIPE DOWN AND CLEAN
- [ ] DUST LAMPS AND LAMPSHADES IN ALL ROOMS
- [ ] CLEAN WINDOW TREATMENTS

THURSDAY

- [ ] WASH HARD FLOORS THROUGHOUT HOUSE
- [ ] CLEAN ALL BATHROOM COUNTERS AND CABINETS
- [ ] CLEAN ALL TOILETS
- [ ] CLEAN ALL TUBS AND SHOWERS

FRIDAY

- [ ] WASH WINDOWS
- [ ] CLEAN WINDOW TREATMENTS
- [ ] ROTATE MATTRESSES
- [ ] WASH ALL BEDDING

SATURDAY

- [ ] DUST AND CLEAN ALL FURNITURE
- [ ] CLEAR NIGHTSTAND AND DRESSER
- [ ] VACUUM WHOLE HOUSE
- [ ] SPOT-CLEAN WALLS

The 31-Day Cleaning Plan

Working 15 to 30 minutes a day, you can get your whole house clean in just a month. This is a great list if you are overwhelmed with your current state of messiness, but want to start somewhere. Just do a little bit every day. If you miss a day, just start where you left off.

☐ DAY 1 Use an extendable duster, dust all edges and corners

☐ DAY 2 Vacuum or wash all vents

☐ DAY 3 Vacuum all edges (where baseboards touch floors)

☐ DAY 4 Wash ½ of baseboards

☐ DAY 5 Wash ½ of baseboards

☐ DAY 6 Using a disinfecting wipe, wipe all switches and plates

☐ DAY 7 Using a disinfecting wipe, wipe all doorknobs

☐ DAY 8 Wash or dust ½ of light fixtures

☐ DAY 9 Wash or dust ½ of light fixtures

☐ DAY 10 Dust any ceiling fans

☐ DAY 11 Clean refrigerator and freezer (wash shelves + bins)

☐ DAY 12 Clean oven and microwave (inside and out)

☐ DAY 13 Clean dishwasher

☐ DAY 14 Remove items from kitchen counters and wash

☐ DAY 15 Clean pantry or food storage (discard expired items)

☐ DAY 16 Organize pantry/food storage

☐ DAY 17 Remove items and wipe out kitchen drawers

☐ DAY 18 Remove items and wipe out kitchen cupboards

☐ DAY 19 Clean laundry room (vacuum, clean washer/dryer)

☐ DAY 20 Wash ½ of windows

☐ DAY 21 Wash ½ of windows

☐ DAY 22 Wash all windowsills

☐ DAY 23 Clean window treatments

☐ DAY 24 Deep clean bathrooms (toilets, counters, shower. . .)

☐ DAY 25 Deep clean bedrooms (bedding, wipe surfaces)

☐ DAY 26 Deep clean living areas (wipe down all surfaces)

☐ DAY 27 Clean carpets and throw rugs

☐ DAY 28 Vacuum all floors

☐ DAY 29 Wash all hard surface floors

☐ DAY 30 Scrub all sinks (use an abrasive cleaner)

☐ DAY 31 Catchall (complete any unfinished tasks)

The Deep-Cleaning Checklist

If you want to do a deep cleaning of your house but have no idea how long it's going to take or how much time you have to commit, try using this deep-cleaning checklist. No time frames, just checkmarks to be made!

- ☐ Using an extendable duster, dust all edges and corners
- ☐ Vacuum or remove and wash all vents
- ☐ Vacuum all edges (where baseboards touch floors)
- ☐ Wash baseboards
- ☐ Wipe down walls — spot-clean for fingerprints and smudges
- ☐ Using a disinfecting wipe, wipe all switches and plates
- ☐ Using a disinfecting wipe, wipe all doorknobs
- ☐ Wash or dust light fixtures and ceiling fans
- ☐ Clean refrigerator and freezer (wipe shelves, wash bins)
- ☐ Clean oven and microwave (inside and out)
- ☐ Clean dishwasher
- ☐ Remove items from kitchen counters and wash counters
- ☐ Clean pantry or food storage (throw away expired items)
- ☐ Organize pantry/food storage

- ☐ Remove items and wipe out all kitchen drawers
- ☐ Remove items and wipe out upper kitchen cupboards
- ☐ Remove items and wipe out lower kitchen cupboards
- ☐ Wipe fronts of kitchen cabinet doors and knobs
- ☐ Clean laundry room (vacuum, wipe down washer/dryer)
- ☐ Wash windows
- ☐ Wash all windowsills
- ☐ Clean window treatments — blinds, curtains, draperies
- ☐ Deep clean bathrooms (toilets, counters, showers/tubs)
- ☐ Deep clean bedrooms (wash bedding, clean all surfaces)
- ☐ Deep clean living areas (wipe down/ dust all surfaces)
- ☐ Wax or oil furniture
- ☐ Clean carpets and throw rugs
- ☐ Vacuum all floors
- ☐ Wash all hard surface floors

DATE STARTED:

DATE COMPLETED:

Pretreating Stain Removal Guide

This chart is for items that are washable. Treat stain as recommended and toss in the washing machine.

STAIN	TREATMENT
Blood and Vomit	Blot with cold water and treat with Homemade Oxygen Bleach Paste (see Chapter 5) made into a paste or added to the washing machine.
Chocolate	Wet with warm water and dab with the Tea Tree Stain Stick (see Chapter 5).
Fruit	Wet area with warm water and dab with white vinegar. If stain remains, rinse and add a little hydrogen peroxide to the stain.
Grass	Pretreat with the Tea Tree Stain Stick or the Lemon and Lavender Liquid Laundry Soap (see Chapter 5 for both recipes). Wash with the hottest setting on your washing machine.
Gum	Place an ice cube on the gum or place the article of clothing in the freezer. Scrape off with a credit card and wash as usual.
Lip Gloss and Lipstick	Dab with rubbing alcohol and soak in Homemade Oxygen Bleach Paste (see Chapter 5). Launder as usual.
Oil and Grease	Rub with a piece of chalkboard chalk to absorb the oil (keep a stick in your laundry room), and/or pretreat with the Stain Spray—General (see Chapter 5).
Pen and Ink	Rinse with cool water. If stain remains, dab with rubbing alcohol or pretreat with Stain Spray—General (see Chapter 5) and wash as usual.

STAIN	TREATMENT
Sweat and Perspiration	Using a 2:1 ratio, mix a little paste of baking soda and white vinegar. If you're working through a stack of T-shirts, you'll want to use about ½ cup of baking soda and about ¼ cup of white vinegar to cover those pit stains. Scrub into stain with a scrub brush or toothbrush. Soak and launder on hottest setting with Homemade Oxygen Bleach Paste and Lemon and Clove Powdered Laundry Soap (see Chapter 5 for both recipes).
Tea and Coffee	Pretreat with Stain Spray—General or Tea Tree Stain Stick (see Chapter 5 for both recipes), soak, and wash as usual.
Tomato Sauce	Dab with cool water. If stain remains, rub a little castile soap into the stain. Let sit for a few minutes and wash as usual.
Water-Based Paint	Simply rinse using warm water while paint is still wet.
Wine	Dab with water and soak up stain. If stain remains, dab with a little vodka or rubbing alcohol and wash as usual.

Notes

METRIC CONVERSION CHART

VOLUME CONVERSIONS

U.S. Volume Measure	Metric Equivalent
⅛ teaspoon	0.5 milliliter
¼ teaspoon	1 milliliter
½ teaspoon	2 milliliters
1 teaspoon	5 milliliters
½ tablespoon	7 milliliters
1 tablespoon (3 teaspoons)	15 milliliters
2 tablespoons (1 fluid ounce)	30 milliliters
¼ cup (4 tablespoons)	60 milliliters
⅓ cup	90 milliliters
½ cup (4 fluid ounces)	125 milliliters
⅔ cup	160 milliliters
¾ cup (6 fluid ounces)	180 milliliters
1 cup (16 tablespoons)	250 milliliters
1 pint (2 cups)	500 milliliters
1 quart (4 cups)	1 liter (about)

WEIGHT CONVERSIONS

U.S. Weight Measure	Metric Equivalent
½ ounce	15 grams
1 ounce	30 grams
2 ounces	60 grams
3 ounces	85 grams
¼ pound (4 ounces)	115 grams
½ pound (8 ounces)	225 grams
¾ pound (12 ounces)	340 grams
1 pound (16 ounces)	454 grams

INDEX

ABOUT THE AUTHOR

Becky Rapinchuk is a cleaning and housekeeping expert, a wife to a wonderful husband and mom to three adorable children, a successful business owner (Clean Mama Printables), and a former art teacher. With an affinity to homekeeping and cleaning, her story began years ago when she was figuring out the best way keep her messy art classroom clean and organized. The tricks she developed easily translated to keeping her home clean, but the real Clean Mama started when her oldest was a baby, and all of a sudden everything seemed to pose a chemical or germ threat to her crawling baby. That was when she started looking for natural and organic ways to really clean her home while protecting her family from toxins. After years of searching for the perfect cleaning product line, she also found that she could make her own effective cleaning products with a few easy-to-find ingredients. That's where this book comes in—it's the culmination of Becky's love for real-world cleaning routines and safe, natural cleaning products. You can find Becky blogging at her website, Cleanmama.net, where she is always looking for new ways to do the mundane tasks of cleaning and organizing and bringing a little more fun into the process. Her focus is natural cleaning, cleaning routines, simple organizing tips, and homekeeping and home management. She has been featured on Oprah.com, *HGTV Magazine*, BHG.com, *Huffington Post*, Answers .com (housekeeping expert), and has also provided cleaning content for Scotch-Brite (3M), Peapod/Reckitt, and Cafemom.com, to name a few.